SEX IN CYBERSPACE

Sex in Cyberspace
Men Who Pay For Sex

SARAH EARLE
The Open University, UK

KEITH SHARP
The University of Gloucestershire, UK

ASHGATE

Published by
Ashgate Publishing Limited
Gower House
Croft Road
Aldershot
Hampshire GU11 3HR
England

Ashgate Publishing Company
Suite 420
101 Cherry Street
Burlington, VT 05401-4405
USA

Ashgate website: http://www.ashgate.com

British Library Cataloguing in Publication Data
Earle, Sarah, 1972-
   Sex in cyberspace : men who pay for sex
   1. PunterNet (Firm) 2. Men - Sexual behavior
   3. Prostitution 4. Sex - Electronic discussion groups
   I. Title II. Sharp, Keith
   306.7'081

Library of Congress Cataloging-in-Publication Data
Earle, Sarah, 1972-
   Sex in cyberspace : men who pay for sex / by Sarah Earle and Keith Sharp.
      p. cm.
   Includes bibliographical references and index.
   ISBN 978-0-7546-3669-4
   1. Men--Sexual behavior. 2. Computer sex. 3. Prostitution. 4. Prostitutes'
customers. I. Sharp, Keith, 1965- II. Title.

   HQ28.E27 2007
   306.740285467'80810941--dc22

                                                                    2006032972
ISBN: 978-0-7546-3669-4

Printed and bound in Great Britain by TJ International Ltd, Padstow, Cornwall.

Contents

Acknowledgements

We would like to thank everybody who has encouraged us with this project or read drafts of earlier chapters: in particular, Gayle Letherby, Carl May and Cathy Lloyd. We would also like to thank our publisher and editors for their patience and for their support.

Glossary

69	Simultaneous fellatio and cunnilingus
A/A-levels	Anal sex
Anal	Using the rectum for sexual intercourse
Around the world	Kissing the entire body before sex
AW0	Anal without a condom
Bareback	Sex without a condom
BBBJ	Bareback blow job
BJ Blow job	Fellatio
Blow job	The act of oral intercourse
Bring off	Ejaculation in the male
Brown	To perform anal intercourse
CIM	Come in mouth
Clit	The clitoris
Completion	Orgasm; OWO to completion means until you cum
Cowgirl	Position for sexual intercourse – man on back, woman on top
Covered	With a condom
Cum	Semen
Doggie style	Position for sexual intercourse – woman on her knees, man entering from behind
Eat	To perform oral intercourse
Facial	Ejaculate over person's face
Fanny	Vagina; pussy; cunny; quim
FR	Field report, a written report of an experience with a sex worker by a client
French	French sex; fellatio
FS	Sometimes means full sex/sexual intercourse but sometimes means full service
Full service	Generally means sexual intercourse with oral sex
Full sex	Vaginal intercourse
FWO	French without (a condom); OWO; BBBJ
GFE	The sex worker providing a girlfriend type experience
Give head	To perform oral intercourse
Go down on	To perform oral intercourse
Hand job	Masturbation
Hobby	The 'hobby' is punting
Hobbyist	Euphemism for a man who frequents sex workers
Horny	Sexually aroused; passionate
HR	Hand relief; same as HJ
Incall	Where the client visits the sex worker. Opposite of outcall
Jack off/jerk off	To masturbate
Lay	To perform sexual intercourse

Load	The fluid from an ejaculation
Massage parlour	Usually a brothel
MFS	Massage and full sex
Mish	Missionary position
O/O-levels	Oral sex
Old dirt road	Using the anus for intercourse
Oral	Oral sex; fellatio; cunnilingus
Outcall	Where the sex worker visits client's home or hotel. Opposite of incall
OWO	Oral without (a condom); FWO; BBBJ
Pearl necklace	This is where you ejaculate over a woman's breasts/shoulders/neck
Pro	A prostitute/sex worker
Provider	A prostitute/sex worker
Punter	A prostitute's/sex worker's client
Reverse	Means the opposite way round to that which is most common between a sex worker and her client. For example, 'reverse oral' means cunnilingus and 'reverse massage' means the client massaging the sex worker
Rim/rimming	When one person licks and kisses their partner's anus like oral sex on a female, except to the anus instead of the vagina
Rubber	A condom
Russian	A tit fuck
Sandwich	Another term for DP
Sixty-nine	Genital oral intercourse performed on each other simultaneously by two partners
Spoons	A position for sexual intercourse – both partners lying on their side, with the man behind the woman
Straight sex	Vaginal intercourse
Suck off	To perform oral intercourse on the penis
Swallows	Means that ejaculate is swallowed
SWO	Sex without (a condom); BBF
Tongue	(verb) To perform oral intercourse
Uncovered	Without a condom
VFM	Value for money
Walk-up	Type of establishment common in Soho. A walk-up has an open door leading into a flat (or two or three). Advertised mainly by means of a note by the entrance saying 'model' and usually giving some details
WG	Working girl; prostitute; escort; sex worker
With	Often means 'with a condom'
Without	Often means 'without a condom'
Working girl	Sex worker or prostitute

Source: Adapted from www.punternet.com

Chapter 1

Men, Sex Work and Society

Men who Pay for Sex

It is commonly said that 'prostitution' is one of the 'oldest professions' and if this cliché is to be believed, then there must, also, be a long history of those who have been willing to pay for sex. Whilst not suggesting that sex work is a single trans-historical and trans-cultural activity (Scambler and Scambler, 1997) it seems fair to argue that within contemporary western societies, paying for sex is both a discreditable and a discrediting activity and those involved in selling sex, or indeed those involved in any aspect of the sex industry, are on the whole considered deviant (Sharp and Earle, 2003).

Whilst there is a considerable body of literature dealing with the experiences of female and male sex workers (Walkowitz, 1980; Chapkis, 1997; McKeganey and Barnard, 1997; Sanders, 2005), there exists comparatively little research on men who pay for sex, particularly within the context of the United Kingdom (UK). Indeed, Perkins (1991) has estimated that less than 1 per cent of all studies of sex work focus on men who pay for sex. The reasons for this are obvious.

Firstly, it is the women who sell sex that have been traditionally perceived as 'the problem', rather than her pimps or punters. Historical analyses of sex work show that it is women who have been, and still are, subject to surveillance and regulation. As such, female sex workers have become the most visible within both lay and professional discourses on sex work (Weitzer, 2000). Secondly, and with notably few exceptions, paying for sex remains amongst the most discreditable and potentially stigmatising of activities in which men can engage within the modern western world, and elsewhere. Also, although sex workers are easily located – on the streets, in parlours or walk ups, via calling-cards left in telephone booths and, more recently, on the net – in contrast, men who pay for sex are less readily located and it has been difficult for researchers to find men willing to participate in social research. The research that has been carried out in the UK has tended to rely either on self-selecting samples – such as men who answer newspaper advertisements – or those recruited through departments of genito-urinary medicine (GUM). In other countries different methods have been used and these are discussed more fully in the next Chapter; for example, Monto's (2000) study of men who pay for sex in the United States relied on a rehabilitation programme for 'Johns'. The limitations of each of these approaches are readily apparent.

The research which forms the basis of this book takes a different approach. Instead of relying on finding samples of men willing to speak of their encounters, it is based on a study of a British internet site – *PunterNet.com* – containing reviews (or 'Field Reports') of men's sexual encounters with female sex workers. We define this as a type of covert cyber-ethnography and as Fox and Roberts suggest 'just as a traditional ethnographer would document a community or other cultural form ... so cyber-ethnographers will document a virtual social world' (1999, p.650). *PunterNet* invites reviews of commercial (predominantly hetero) sex between adults or what Scambler (1997) describes as 'voluntary adult sex work'. It does not include accounts of sex work on the streets and it must be recognized that there are likely to be considerable differences between so-called 'indoor' and 'outdoor' sex work (Plumridge, 2001). Previous research suggests that outdoor sex workers are more likely to experience physical and sexual assault from punters, are more likely to be under the surveillance and regulation of the police, and most likely work for lower wages than the majority of indoor sex workers. There is also some evidence to suggest that outdoor sex workers are more likely to practise unsafe sex with clients, and more likely to use drugs. We also acknowledge that other forms of sex work exist including that which is coerced and that involving children. For example, Brown's (2000) harrowing account of trafficking in Asia depicts stories of sexual slavery in which girls and young women are bought, sold and kept prisoner often until such time as they die of HIV/AIDS, drug addiction, alcoholism or other diseases of poverty. Brown states:

> All over the world women are sold, tricked, forced or lured into prostitution. They are incarcerated in brothels and girls who are little more than children are compelled to service innumerable clients. They are unable to refuse the customers and unable to escape from brothels that are nothing but prisons (Brown, 2000, p.1).

Malarek's (2003) text also describes the experiences of the nameless 'Natashas'; young women smuggled out of Eastern Europe under false promises of employment as nannies, models or domestics in other countries, only to find, however, that they have been trafficked into sex work and that they 'owe' money which they are unlikely ever to be able to repay. Jeffreys (1997) also provides a useful historical and political overview of the global trafficking of women. However, the remit of this book does not extend to such forms of trafficking and sexual slavery, as far as we are aware. The more specialist markets of bondage, domination, discipline and correction are also not represented here although some of the men described within this book do occasionally refer to engaging in role play and uniforms. We also acknowledge that other scholars do not accept the distinction between the different forms of sex work that we have identified here. For example, in a critical account of the role of non-governmental organisations in condemning violence against women, Raymond argues:

> The philosophy that prostitution is a human right has been advanced in international forums ... by drawing distinctions between forced and free, adult and child, third world and first world prostitution, and between prostitution and trafficking. These distinctions are then used to make some forms of prostitution acceptable and legitimate, revising the

harm that is done to women in prostitution into a consenting act and excluding prostitution from the category of violence against women. The sex industry thrives on this language and these distinctions (Raymond, 1998, p.1).

Leaving these debates to one side for a moment, we argue that paying for sex is, potentially, a deeply discrediting activity for men, not only in terms of risk to social identity but in relation to the risk to self-identity. Within this context, 'risk' therefore takes one of two forms. First is the obvious risk of being seen in a 'red light zone' or caught paying for sex. We know very little about the men who pay for sex – or the punters – in the UK or, indeed, elsewhere. Confidential questionnaires used in the National Survey of Sexual Attitudes and Lifestyles (Johnson and Mercer, 2001) reported that nearly 9 per cent of men in London had paid-for sex and that these were aged between 16 and 44 years, with a nationwide figure of 4.3 per cent. Wellings *et al.*, (1994) have argued that men are more likely to visit a sex worker as they get older and state that over 10 per cent of the male population aged 45-59 years old admit to buying sex. It would also appear that many punters have wives, partners, or girlfriends and would not wish their activities to become known to them (McKeganey and Barnard, 1996). Hester and Westmarland (2004) have suggested that the typical client is married. The second risk threatens a core feature of an assumed hegemonic heterosexual masculinity – namely, that men are sexually attractive to women and capable of attracting women as sexual partners. Rightly, or wrongly, an obvious implication of paying for sex is precisely that a man is incapable of attracting women in this way. Given these considerable risks, the way that men present themselves in cyberspace offers an opportunity to examine the way in which men who pay for sex manage their engagement in deviance and (potentially) deviant sexual identities.

Sex Work and the Regulation of the Female Body

Sex work is unique in that it has been seen both to constitute a social problem and to be the solution to a social problem. Historically, and to date, sex work has been associated with the transmission of illness and disease. It has also been seen as a utilitarian outlet for men's sexual 'frustrations', without which such frustrations would otherwise lead to the rape of 'innocent' women and children. Within some contexts it has also served the purpose of the sexual initiation of young men and others with whom 'nice', 'normal' women would not wish to have sex (for example, the ugly, the impaired or the very old). As Wilton argues, 'prostitution' has been described in many ways:

> a pathology, a disorder of sexual function ... a form of or consequence of intellectual impairment .... a criminal activity ... or a form of immorality ... as 'foul sewers' ... 'seminal drains' ... or bridgeheads of HIV infection (Wilton, 1999, p.189).

The regulation of women's sexuality, particularly the regulation of the bodies of female sex workers is long-standing (O'Neill, 2001). There are many examples of this in recorded history, some of them in the distant past, such as the regulation of medieval brothels (Mazo-Karras, 1989), others more recent, for example, the regulation of women in tolerance zones in the Netherlands (see, for example, Drobler, 1991).

In an account of women's sexuality in Somerset, England in the early Seventeenth Century, Quaife (1979) outlines the regulation of women's sexuality outside of marriage. All but monogamous married women could be defined as 'unruly women'; these included the 'wayward widows', the 'consenting spinsters', the 'adulterous wife', and the 'prostitute'. According to Quaife the promiscuous activity of these women was widespread and could fall into any one of four categories. Firstly, there was the 'vagrant whore' – a woman of little means who wandered from parish to parish soliciting wherever she could. Secondly, Quaife refers to the 'public whore', who operated from a particular inn or bawdy house. The third category was the 'private whore' who gave her services to one or two men over a specific period of time, before moving on. The fourth type was the 'village whore', 'who ranged from the slut to the almost respectable protector of the chastity and fidelity of other village women' (p.146). We can see here some parallels with different forms of contemporary sex work: street work, escort work, and work in parlours, walk-ups and saunas. We can also see parallels with the contemporary double standard of sexual behaviour for men and women. As Holland, Ramazanoglu, Sharpe and Thomson state '... the same sexual attitudes, desires and behaviour by men and by women have different meanings, resulting in different sexual reputations' (1998, p.173). For example, in their study of young people, heterosexuality and power, one young woman is quoted as saying *'If you sleep around you're a slag, if a bloke sleeps around he's lucky'*. And, as they rightly note, whilst this double standard distinguishes between what is appropriate both for men and women, it is really the behaviour of women that is harshly judged.

Studies of sex work in the Eighteenth Century also show parallels between women working as 'prostitutes' and other women. Henderson's (1999) account of prostitution in London, for example, suggests that women moved fairly seamlessly between prostitution and other forms of low status work. He details the relentless policing and regulation of female prostitutes, both on the streets and in brothels. For example, around 1735, local watch committees were established with the purpose of regulating street prostitutes. Henderson's work shows, however, two very distinct images of prostitution in the Eighteenth Century. The first image depicts the prostitute as an agent of destruction who, through her actions, was able to foul society, 'spreading physical ruin and moral disintegration' (pp.166-7). In the second image, which is the direct reverse of this, the prostitute is seen as victim and her entry into prostitution and her decision to remain there are presented as involuntary.

In Acton's (1972) work on prostitution in the late Nineteenth Century, first published in 1870, distinction is also made between two different types of prostitute. The first class of women he describes as the 'kept mistresses' – 'a more reserved class of prostitutes' (p.1). The second class he describes as 'common street-walkers'.

According to Acton, prostitution was ineradicable and he believed that English society should embrace the prevention and regulation of prostitution.

As part of this prevention and regulation, the Contagious Diseases Act, operating in Garrison towns, allowed a justice of the peace to detain a 'common prostitute' (the definition of which was much debated) and subject her to periodical medical examination for the purpose of ascertaining whether she was infected with contagious disease. Beds were secured at the Victorian Lock Hospitals with the objective of treatment, as well as moral and religious instruction. In a visit to one such hospital, Acton concludes that: 'Their disease appears to be entirely local, both in origin and character. It arises, as I believe, in the great majority of cases, simply from the continual irritation and excitement of the generative organs consequent upon their mode of life, although it may be caused, no doubt, occasionally by direct contagion from urethral discharges in the male' (p.86). Here we have an example of the way in which the female prostitute was firmly believed to be the source of contagion, and the regulation of female sexuality, rather than male desire, was the norm.

In an account of prostitution during the First World War, a similar picture is depicted. Writing about the increasing dangers of prostitution during this time and the inevitability of male sexual desire and promiscuity, Fischer and Dubois suggest:

> Indeed, the only effective way of obviating the danger inherent in casual sexual contacts would have been, as someone has ironically observed, to castrate every soldier before putting him into uniform. But to examine this more or less jocular argument – and this does not mean that we ourselves are treating the subject in that spirit – this solution would have been disastrous, for eunuchs are not exactly ideal warriors. Warriors and male are two inseparable concepts, and the term male necessarily implies sexual activity (Fischer and Dubois, 1937, p.323).

Whilst we have but offered a flavour of the history of sex work here, we can see how sex work has been understood as both a 'necessary evil' and a social, legal and medical problem. Public concerns have centred on the regulation of women and women's sexuality, rather than on male desire and demand. Thus, the men who pay for sex have remained largely invisible within the literature and within the history of sex work.

Prostitution, or 'Sex "Work"'?

Considerable attention has been given in recent years to the status and definition of sex work. There is extensive literature dealing with this issue, which we believe is best understood and described as the continuum of sex/work/abuse. Three questions are central to this continuum: Is sex work 'just sex'? Is sex work 'ordinary' work? Or, is sex work an abuse of women? Whilst there is no consensus on the nature of sex work, we briefly outline some of the debates below.

Is Sex Work 'Just Sex'?

It is widely accepted within sex research today that sex is not a 'natural' act (Tiefer, 1995) but one that must be understood within a sociocultural context. This context determines what counts as sex and the meanings we attribute to where, when, why, how and with whom one has sex. We could argue that sex work is 'just sex', except that women are getting paid for it. This argument has two main advantages. Firstly, it serves to deconstruct the false dichotomy between 'normal', as opposed to 'abnormal' sexual behaviour and, for this, read consensual non-commercial heterosex in contrast to commercial sex. Consequently, this serves to destigmatize sex workers and the men who pay for sex. Prior research on the dominant discourses around consensual non-commercial heterosex suggests that three discourses are especially apparent: male sexual drive discourse, a permissive discourse, and a discourse of reciprocity (Gavey, McPhillips and Braun, 1999; Braun, Gavey and McPhillips, 2003). These discourses are echoed within men's accounts of paying for sex.

Secondly, if we argue that sex work is just sex then we recognize the power relations inherent in all sexual contracts. The research by Holland, Ramazanoglu, Sharpe and Thomson (1998), for example, clearly shows the playing out of power and control in the sexual relationships of young women and men. Indeed, it has been argued that sex work is one of the few social contexts in which women, rather than men, are able to negotiate the terms of their sexual encounters (Warr and Pyett, 1999). However, research on sex workers and first person accounts of sex work are mixed. Whilst for some women sex work is just like any other kind of sex, for others sex work is very different to the private sex of their non-commercial intimate relationships.

Is Sex Work Ordinary 'Work'?

In the 1970s, pro-prostitution prostitutes' rights organisations began to promote the idea that prostitution was work, and should be seen as such. Organisations, such as the American COYOTE (Call Off Your Old Tired Ethics), argued that being paid for an hour of sexual services was no different to being paid for an hour's typing. The idea of sex work as ordinary work has developed considerable currency since then. Chapkis (1997, p.76), for example, argues: 'Once sex and emotion have been stripped of their unique relationship to nature and the self, it no longer automatically follows that their alienation or commodification is simply and necessarily destructive'. For Pheterson (1996) the promotion of sex work as work serves to counter the 'whore stigma' which has shaped and defined women who sell sex as dirty and bad. More recently, Brewis and Linstead have argued:

> Many responses to prostitution have tended to focus on the *sex* aspect rather than the *work* aspect, which constructs prostitution as a personal quality, part of the identity of the individual ... we view prostitution as a work activity, as a job that people do, alongside many other more 'normal' activities which are not held to be definitive of their identity ...

Sex work is work and needs to be seen as such. It is economically and socially important to all of the societies in which it occurs (Brewis and Linstead, 2002, p.309).

It follows then, that within this context, sex work is just a job like any other and sex workers are like any other employees. Thus, sex workers should be entitled to the same rights and legal protection afforded to workers within other industries. Pyle (2001) notes that increasing numbers of women have migrated domestically and internationally in order to earn money within a largely restructured global economy. In her analysis of gendered global production networks she compares the numbers of women who have become sex workers, maids or domestics and argues that the growth of women in such networks is characterized by considerable risk and lack of security. Moreover, she argues that the development and maintenance of gendered global production networks is in the interests of many governments.

Many writers, activists and researchers would agree that sex work is work. Most importantly, women working in the sex industry use the language of trade and commerce to describe what they do when they exchange sex for money; they refer to sex work as the 'business' and to men who pay for sex as 'clients' or 'punters'. Indeed, Mistress L, a London sex worker states:

Sex work is one of the few industries where women can earn far in excess of their male cohorts and this fact alone can make it very empowering for women. It offers them flexible hours, excellent money in a safe and female-friendly environment (Mistress L, 2001, p.148).

Is Sex Work an Abuse of Women?

Whilst the debate on sex work has changed over the years, and continues to evolve, for some writers their standpoint on the sex/work/abuse continuum, in favour of an approach which defines all sex work as abuse, is definitive and immovable. Many of the more recent texts have developed such a standpoint on the basis of research focusing on the trafficking of women and children across international borders. Jeffreys, for example, makes her position clear when she argues that 'prostitution' is, universally, 'a form of brutal cruelty on the part of men that constitutes a violation of women's human rights, wherever and however it takes place' (1997, p.348). However, whilst Jeffreys' work is convincing in places it is, like the work of some other writers, based on political conviction rather than empirical evidence; we are not convinced that such a universal position on sex work can be defended as there are many women working in different parts of the sex industry and for different reasons and, thus, the empirical evidence is mixed. Even first person accounts of sex work, such as that of Martina Keogh (2003) – which portrays a harrowing account of neglect, abuse and 'prostitution' in Dublin – do not depict sex work in the uni-dimensional way that writers such as Jeffreys, and others, would have us believe. Others writers present a less monolithic perspective on sex work. Wood (2000), for example, whilst still maintaining a standpoint which defines sex work as abuse, argues that power needs to be understood as a contested and negotiated resource which is enacted through interaction.

It is also worth considering the perspective put forward by Malarek who suggests that women who have been trafficked cannot always be easily distinguished from those who have not: 'To the casual observer, they blend in seamlessly with the women who have *chosen* to exchange money for sex' (2003, pp.3-4). Here, at least, Malarek acknowledges the possibility of difference between women who have been trafficked, and other women who might choose to earn a living selling sex. Whilst we suspect that the majority of women depicted in men's cyber accounts have chosen to work in this industry, we cannot categorically rule out the possibility that some of these women have not.

What is essentially at stake is the question of women's agency. As Simmons (1998) suggests whether one believes that sex work is an occupational choice, or, a non-consensual one is based on the level of analysis adopted. At one level, if sex work is defined and understood as ordinary work then sex workers are perceived as choosing to work in this industry: arguably, such proponents are concerned with the choices of *individual* women. However, if one believes that sex work is an abuse, then *all* women who work in this industry are compelled to do so by social circumstance. At this level, such proponents are concerned with the *institution* of 'prostitution', rather than the act itself.

Men, Masculinity and Self-Identity

A Reflexive Project of the Self

The literature on self-identity is vast and varied. We do not attempt a comprehensive discussion of this here but only review that which is most relevant for our immediate purposes. We begin with a review of the subject provided by Jenkins (1996) who makes a valid point when he suggests that the concept of self-identity is constituted of two distinct features: process and reflexivity. His discussion of these leads him to propose the following definition of self-identity as:

> an individual's reflexive sense of her or his own particular identity, constituted *vis à vis* others ... without which we would not know who we are and hence would not be able to act (Jenkins, 1996, pp.29-30).

If we accept his definition then we accept that self-identity develops through interaction between self and others. In doing so we should therefore consider two fundamental premises: (1) the extent to which self-identity is a continuously revised phenomenon, and (2) the extent to which the individual is actively engaged in its construction. According to the first premise, the construction of self-identity has no 'end'; that is, self-identity is continuously revised (Marshall, 1996). Subsequently, one must also assume that self-identity is constructed rather than pre-given, or fixed. Giddens' (1991) concept of ontological security also contributes to an understanding of self-identity as a continuously revised phenomenon. Whilst ontological security refers to the way in which an individual can have certainty in who they are and in the world around them, ontological insecurity is created through uncertainty and risk. In this book, we argue that paying for sex is an uncertain business which poses risks to identity and to the maintenance of ontological security. According to the second premise, self-identity is a reflexive process in which the individual is actively engaged in the construction of self-identity. This has two significant implications: first, for the way in which punters may regard themselves as both object and subject and, second, for the way in which punters can be seen as rational in the presentation of the self in the accounts they write for *PunterNet*.

Taking each of these points in turn, the first refers to the notion that 'social interaction rests upon a taking of oneself and others into account' (Meltzer, Petras and Reynolds, 1975, p.1). In the process of being able to construct self-identity, the individual must not only be able to reflect on himself but must also be able to reflect on how others might see him. Cooley's (1964) concept of the 'looking-glass self' is an important contribution to this debate. He argues that individuals must be able to see themselves as objects:

> As we see our face, figure, and dress in the glass, and are interested in them because they are ours, and pleased or otherwise with them accordingly as they do or do not answer to what we should like them to be; so in imagination we perceive in another's mind some thought of our appearance, manners, aims, deeds, character, friends, and so on, and are variously affected by it (Cooley, 1964, p.184).

Many writers can be criticized for ignoring the context within which individuals engage with the looking-glass self, particularly with regard to gender relations. Feminist writers have paid a great deal of attention to this issue and have argued that women (in particular) are objectified within modern western societies. MacSween, for example, has argued that women, 'are obliged to produce [themselves] as adequate and acceptable "spectacles", as objects external to their selves' whereas men, traditionally, have not (1993, p.174).

The second point which warrants clarification is the extent to which the individual is rational in the construction of self-identity. Goffman's contribution to this debate is well documented. For example, in *The Presentation of Self in Everyday Life* Goffman (1959) discusses the way in which the individual, through interaction, presents an image of him/herself to others. He argues that,

> Sometimes the individual will act in a thoroughly calculating manner, expressing himself in a given way solely in order to give the kind of impression to others that is likely to evoke from them a specific response he is concerned to obtain (Goffman, 1959, p.6).

Giddens' discussion of lifestyles is also useful, and underpinned by the work of Goffman, amongst others, he suggests:

> The reflexive project of the self, which consists of the sustaining of coherent, yet continuously revised, biographical narratives, takes place in the context of multiple

choice as filtered through abstract systems ... individuals are forced to negotiate lifestyle choices among a diversity of options ... because of the 'openness' of social life today, the pluralisation of context of action and the diversity of 'authorities', lifestyle choice is increasingly important in the constitution of self-identity (Giddens, 1991, p.5).

Jenkins' (1996) description of self-identity as a reflexive process is supported by Giddens' account of the reflexive project of the self. It is a convincing account of self-identity and one which acknowledges the dual nature of individual behaviour in terms of agency and structure. It is also one based on the assumption that individuals are both determined by and determiners of society, as Meltzer, Petras and Reynolds suggest:

> ... the individual and society are inseparable units. While it may be possible to separate the two units analytically, the underlying assumption is that a complete understanding of either one demands a complete understanding of the other. Coupled with this assumption is the belief that the inseparability of the individual and society is defined in terms of a mutually interdependent relationship, not a one-sided, deterministic one (Meltzer, Petras and Reynolds, 1975, p.2).

Mead (1934) uses the concept of sociality to refer to the existence of individuals in dual systems and refers to the role of the 'generalized other' in the construction of self-identity. He argues:

> ... the individual takes the attitude of the generalized other toward himself, without reference to its expression in any particular other individuals; and in concrete thought he takes that attitude in so far as it is expressed in the attitudes towards his behaviour of those other individuals with whom he is involved in the given social situation or act. But only by taking the attitude of the generalized other toward himself, in one or other of these ways, can he think at all ... (Mead, 1934, pp.155-6).

Reflexivity is, thus, a central feature of any attempt to understand self-identity. However, traditional accounts of self-identity have been subject to criticism. Some of these are addressed below.

Gender, Masculinities and Self-identity

Butler (1990) mounts a powerful critique of conventional theories of self-identity by pointing out that an appropriate understanding can only be reached by accepting that identity is gendered. She suggests that any discussion of identity must consider the issue of gender relations since '"persons" only become intelligible through becoming gendered' (p.16). Kimmel (1990) extends this debate, arguing that gender is, in fact, the central organising principle of sexuality.

Theories of men and masculinities take their starting point, in part, from the long history of feminist thought which seeks to understand the nature of gendered identities. In this book we argue that sex and sexuality are central features of a normative hegemonic masculinity, just as mothering and motherhood are features of femininity. In relation to the latter, for example, Battersby (1998, p.16) argues that: '... whether or not a woman is lesbian, infertile, post-menopausal or childless, in modern western cultures she will be assigned a subject-position linked to a body that has perceived potentialities for birth'. Whereas writing about men, Seidler argues:

> Even if a man has never made love to a woman, there is enormous pressure to pretend that he has. Sex is the way we prove our masculinity; it is the moment at which we can feel safe from the challenges of others. So our sexual relations become an arena in which we have to prove ourselves (Seidler, 1989, p.23).

Kimmel (1990) suggests that the male sexual script provides a normative blueprint which determines men's erotic life and constructs masculine identities. Drawing on the work of Brannon and David (1976), he argues for four 'rules of masculinity': (1) The avoidance of all behaviours that remotely suggest the feminine. (2) The importance of success and status in conferring masculinity. (3) Emotional and affective distance. (4) Aggression and risk taking. He argues that whilst these four rules do not capture all masculinities, they specify a normative masculinity against which all masculinities are measured. The contemporary male sexual script, he argues, socially constructs a sexuality that is detached, phallocentric and driven by fantasy. For many writers, masculinity thus serves not only to objectify women, but also to alienate men (for example, see Brod, 1990). For some writers, normative male heterosex represents a continuum of unwanted sexual behaviours that are endured by women from childhood through to adulthood (Patton and Mannison, 1998).

Whilst gender serves as the organizing principle for masculinity, and femininity and masculinity must be understood in relation to one another, masculinity needs to be understood as an 'umbrella term' encompassing heterogeneity of masculinities structured by the categories of class, ethnicity, and age, amongst others. Whitehead argues that it is no longer tenable to talk of masculinity in the singular, 'given recognition of the multiplicity, historicity and dynamism of gender representations' (2002, p.33). Our concern within this book is to explore the way in which *PunterNet* serves to simultaneously create and sustain heterosexual masculinity/ies within the context of a normative community of men who pay for sex.

Punters in Cyberspace

The Net as Social Technology

This book is about men's cyber-accounts of paying for sex and, as such, we now turn to a discussion of punters in cyberspace and to the role of the net as a predominantly social technology. Sproull and Faraj (1997) argue that contemporary discussions of the net are dominated by accounts of individuals who are looking for, and manipulating, information. The net is thus seen as a massive source of knowledge and information to be 'searched' or 'browsed'. However, Sproull and Faraj argue that if we accept that individuals are social actors:

> ... then we should view the net as a social technology [which] allows people with common interests to find each other, talk and listen, and sustain connections over time (Sproull and Faraj, 1997, pp.38-9).

Jewkes and Sharp (2003) rightly argue that the net is a highly gendered social technology. Firstly, because the majority of those who design, develop and distribute the net are men. Secondly, because many of the practices facilitated by the net – hacking, stalking, trafficking, pornography, and so on – are predominantly performed by men and the victims of these practices are usually women and children. Many feminist commentators have agreed with this position and argue that the net provides additional opportunities for (predominantly) men to exploit women and children. For example, writing specifically about pornography, MacKinnon (1995) argues that the net has provided increased opportunities for the distribution of images which serve to exploit and objectify women. She suggests that pornography in cyberspace is just a more technologically sophisticated way of exploiting women which opens new markets, crosses new boundaries and 'pioneers new harms' (p.1959). For those who believe that pornography itself is harmful, then the net does pose a real new threat in that it can be cheaper to produce and distribute and can reach a far wider audience than ever before, thus reducing barriers to both publish and receive (Mehta and Plaza, 1997).

The trade in brides has received similar attention. For example, Butterworth (1993) argues that the net facilitates the rapid publication of information, enabling men to pimp women, and enabling the advance of a global sexual exploitation of women. Whilst the trade in brides is not new, and can be traced back to the nineteenth century at least (Worsnop, 1990) the net perpetuates already existing patterns of inequality and oppression. It is no coincidence, for example, that internet sites offer brides and not husbands. Letherby and Marchbank (2003) suggest that the metaphor of buying a car on-line would not be out of place within the trade of 'mail-order' brides in that: 'Not only can the purchaser select the "model" of woman he seeks ... he can also access all the other necessary business information, in just the same way as he would select a dealer and car loan firm!' (p.70).

Of course the simplistic positioning of men as oppressors and women as victims does not, in any shape or form, underscore our endeavours here. Indeed, as Letherby and Marchbank (2003, p.68) note: 'Oppression and exploitation are not unproblematic concepts and it is too simplistic to argue that women are inevitably oppressed and men the inevitable oppressors'. So-called 'cyber-feminists' have made much of the net's capacity to provide a space for women to come together in which they can 'chatter, natter, work and play' (Plant, 2000, p.325). Others, such as van Zoonen (2002) argue that the internet is as much a feminine and female world as a masculine/male one and that it is essential to look beyond the 'male gaze' in order to understand this. Writing about multi-user games, Turkle (1997) also argues that the net serves as a forum for the construction and reconstruction of gender in virtual realities. And writing about women's use of online pornography, Jewkes and Sharp (2003) discuss the role of the net in subverting the traditionally gendered consumption of pornographic images. In Chapter 3 we explore women's use of the net to advertise themselves and their sexual services. This, we suggest, demonstrates both the gendered subversion of the net by women and their part in the commodification of bodies and sex.

Sexual Stories in Cyberspace

The use of cyberspace as a vehicle for sexual storytelling has the potential to enhance, as well as threaten, the maintenance of masculinity. As we have already argued, the act of paying for sex constitutes a significant threat to the maintenance of conventional masculine identities. Whilst on the face of it, writing about such encounters might seem to further compromise the maintenance of that identity, we suggest that, in the context of a cyber-community such as *PunterNet*, it has a strong identity-maintaining function.

Plummer (1975) has argued that all sexual experience becomes 'socially organized', but makes an important distinction between categories of experience which are collectively supported and those which are not:

> ... all sexual experience becomes socially organized ... Thus the masturbator, the necrophile and the frotteurist will organise their sexual experiences, in the main, without any kind of collective support, whiles 'swingers', homosexuals and premarital lovers are more likely to organise their experiences in group situations with others. Both kinds of sexual experiences become socially organised, but only the latter becomes enmeshed in collectively evolved norms (Plummer, 1975, p.85).

In contrast to providing sexual services for money, and certain other forms of sexual deviance, we would argue that paying for sex, whilst always socially organized, has been organized without any kind of collective support until the emergence of sites such as *PunterNet.com*. Cyberspace and, more specifically, *PunterNet* has afforded the punter a virtual space in which sexual experiences can become both socially organized and, crucially, enmeshed in collectively evolved norms. The punter is, thus, no longer obliged to define his actions only in terms of the prevailing (negative) attitudes to paying for sex (for example, that men who pay for sex are inadequate) but can now do so in relation to, and within, an alternative normative order in which paying for sex is defined as perfectly compatible with a creditable heterosexual masculine identity.

We are not arguing here for a virtual technological utopia, as discussed by Robins (1995), but for the potential technological solution to the problem of sexual deviance, as described by Stone who argues that virtual communities are 'practical adaptations to the real circumstances that confront persons seeking community ... In this context, electronic virtual communities are complex and ingenious strategies for survival' (1991, p.11). In a study of sex talk amongst young boys aged 11 to 16, Kehily suggests:

the collective structure of the male peer group offers a performative space where heterosexuality and masculinity can be fused and displayed. This space can also be seen to provide a forum for a form of secular confessional in which young men disclose details of their sexual encounters with girls. Transforming desire into discourse, in this context, is turned into a boast that seeks valoration rather than repentance (Kehily, 2001, pp.179-80).

And further that:

... sex talk between males serves many purposes and can be seen to have a range of regulatory effects; policing the boundaries of gender-appropriate behaviour for young men and young women, providing an imaginary ideal of desirable masculinity, bolstering the reputation of particular males, concealing vulnerabilities, and producing heterosexual hierarchies (Kehily, 2001, p.180).

In the same way, we argue that the cyberspace provided by *PunterNet* is one in which a particular variant of heterosexual masculinity can be fused and displayed; one in which the apparent contradiction between a positive masculine identity and paying for sex is systematically nullified. In writing and submitting a review, the *PunterNet* author performs his masculinity, and draws upon normative resources which are only available to him within this particular community.

Sex in Cyberspace

In this book we seek to challenge some of the assumptions that have been made elsewhere in the literature, in particular when those assumptions about men who pay for sex have been made with little reference to men's own narratives and have drawn, either wholly or mostly, on the experiences of female sex workers. As Plummer has argued the problem of meaning is central to sociology although the 'question of how an individual gives meaning to his sexuality has been [and continues to be] evaded' (1975, p.7). We stress, as others have before us, the importance of grounding theory in 'the everyday world and not in the armchair' (Plummer, 1975, p.90).

To this end we begin, in Chapter 2, to outline our research methods and explore the implications of this method for our findings. We came across the website *PunterNet. com* several years ago and were intrigued to find that the invisible had been made (partly) visible. Men who pay for sex, who had been traditionally neglected within the study of the sex industry, were sharing their experiences of commercial sex with each other, most probably for the first time. The website offers an insight into the hidden world of men who pay for sex allowing us to explore their normative world through their accounts. However, the findings presented in this book move beyond mere descriptions of men's accounts of commercial sex – what they do where, with whom, for how long, and for how much – towards an analysis of men, sex work and society. Chapter 2 explores the authenticity of men's cyber accounts and introduces the reader to the normative world of *PunterNet.com*.

The purpose of Chapter 3 is two-fold. The first part of this chapter examines the representation of sex work on the internet, focusing particularly on women's own use of the net as a shop window and examines the role of the net in helping to transform social relations between the women who sell sex and the men who pay for it. The second part of this chapter explores men's descriptions of women and the ways in which female bodies are objectified and commodified within sex work.

In Chapter 4, we turn our attention to the issues of intimacy, emotion and romance within the context of paying for sex. The purpose of this chapter is not to determine men's motivations, which has been the driving force within most research on men who pay for sex until now, but to discuss the role played by intimacy, emotional labour and emotion work in the management of a potentially deviant identity. In Chapter 4 we also introduce the concept of 'girlfriend sex', the holy grail of emotional intimacy. Drawing on Goffman's work on the confidence game, and subsequent work on other areas of the sex industry, we also consider whether sex work is a 'con'.

Whilst acknowledging that commercial sex involves the commodification of emotional intimacy – or the development of counterfeit intimacy – in Chapter 5 we argue that physical pleasure and erotic performance are also important elements of the commercial encounter. In this chapter we discuss men's accounts of their own, largely phallocentric, pleasure as well as their accounts of the pleasure they 'give' to female sex workers. Just as non-commercial consensual heterosex is based on the normative assumption of sexual reciprocity, men's accounts of commercial sex echo these normative expectations. Here we focus on men's accounts of female orgasm, the way in which they seek authenticity, and further extend our discussion of sex work as a con.

Whilst the academic literature continues to debate the position of sex work within the continuum of sex/work/abuse, it is clear from men's accounts that the majority believe paying for sex is a commercial transaction. Indeed, as we shall discuss in Chapter 3, this is part of the normative world of *PunterNet.com*. In Chapter 6 we explore the language of trade in which female sex workers are the vendors and men the consumers. We focus specifically on the concepts of power and time and the relationship between trade and value-for-money.

It is our intention within this book to focus solely on men's narratives of paying for sex and to inform and stimulate debate on sex work. Our work follows in a sociological tradition of research which seeks to explore, discuss and understand deviant phenomena, rather than attempt to change it. However, in Chapter 7 we explore our findings within the more contemporary world of sex research, a world which has focused predominantly on public health promotion and HIV/AIDS prevention. This question is, of course, not unique to our research but our methodological approach does raise distinct questions. Furthermore, although practical application in the 'real' world has not been the primary focus of our endeavour we feel that it should be of concern to all those who engage in sociological thinking and research.

Finally, just as Scambler and Scambler (1997, p.xv) have argued for 'the respectful attribution of agency' to be the starting point of research on sex workers we, too, argue for the attribution of agency to any analysis of the men who pay for sex who have, for too long, been portrayed – at best – as 'brainless dicks' and – at worst – as those who brutally use and abuse women and children.

Chapter 2

Researching Sex in Cyberspace

Researching Men who Pay for Sex

This chapter begins by outlining the methodology adopted in our study. It then moves on to consider some of the issues which our approach raises, both for the data we go on to discuss in later chapters and for sociological research more generally.

Whilst data concerning the experiences and perceptions of sex workers and other women working in the sex industry is comparatively easy to come by, the experiences of those (mainly) men who pay for the services of sex workers have traditionally been much harder to research. The reasons for this are fairly obvious. Paying for sexual services is a discreditable activity; discreditable in the sense used by Goffman (1963) to refer to generally invisible deviance which runs the risk of becoming visible and, thus, actually discrediting the individual concerned. Individuals in such discreditable situations have a strong incentive to avoid exposure, and nowhere is this more apparent than in the case of a man who pays for sex. As Soothill and Sanders (2005) note, the sex industry is defined by anonymity and the need to protect identity – this applies to those who sell sex, as well as to those who pay for it. To be identified as someone who pays for sex exposes a man to discredit in a variety of ways and in relation to a range of his relationships. His marriage, or other intimate relationship, is likely to be put at obvious risk by exposure. Equally, his relationships with friends, workmates and social acquaintances are also likely to be jeopardized by such exposure. Exposure as a man who pays for sex invites the labels of 'deviant', 'pervert', 'criminal', 'dangerous' or, perhaps most damaging of all, as repulsive or sexually inadequate.

A second obstacle to finding samples of men who pay for sex is purely practical. Where does one go to find such men? There is no 'sampling frame' – no convenient list of men who pay for sex. Most encounters with sex workers entail taking significant precautions aimed at avoiding exposure. Even if men were, on the whole, willing to talk about their experiences it is far from obvious how one would go about finding and contacting them.

The method we have adopted makes use of a novel technology, the net, and a novel social phenomenon which has arisen from the net – the fact that men, in quite large numbers, post accounts of their experiences with sex workers on publicly accessible websites – to overcome some of the difficulties inherent in researching men who pay for sex. Prior to going on to consider our approach in detail, it is worth reviewing some of the methods which have been adopted by other researchers.

Before the net took off as a medium through which the clients of sex workers exchanged information, methods of acquiring samples of such men were relatively restricted. All suffered significant limitations and researchers were often required to resort to several methods of data collection, since depending on one sole method was often unreliable and unlikely to yield a sufficient number of respondents within a reasonable timescale.

One commonly used method has been to approach clients directly in situations where they are thought to be purchasing sexual services. This has mainly entailed approaching men who are soliciting the services of street workers. Leaving aside the probably unrepresentative nature of street work, the main and, indeed, obvious, drawback of such an approach is that the majority of men will refuse to participate in the research. This was one of the approaches employed by McKeganey and Barnard (1996) in their study of sex workers and their clients in Glasgow. It is not surprising that, despite the sensitive nature of the approach made by the researchers:

> The response was almost always the same, a more or less polite 'get lost' (McKeganey and Barnard, 1996, p.14).

McKeganey (1994) also found that men approached in the street would lie about the purpose for them being there, claiming that they had just stopped to 'catch up on some paperwork'; these men were often seen hours later with a sex worker in their car. Other studies have approached men who visit massage parlours (for example, see Plumridge and Chetwynd's (1996) study of commercial sex in New Zealand). However, these studies are limited in so far as they are reporting on only one form of sex work.

A related avenue, also adopted by McKeganey and Barnard – amongst others (see, also, Campbell, 1998) – is to approach attendees at GUM clinics, and interview them on their contacts with female sex workers. This is usually done via the staff of the clinic, who are asked to enquire whether an attendee has had a recent interaction with a sex worker and, if so, whether they would be prepared to take part in a research study. McKeganey and Barnard report obtaining information from 68 men in this way. However, a number of points need to be made about this approach. Firstly, there is no reason to believe that typical clients of sex workers are significantly more likely than members of the general population to attend GUM clinics. It follows that samples of men obtained in this way are not necessarily likely to be typical of the population of clients as a whole. Secondly samples obtained in this way are still self-selecting: anyone is at liberty to decline the invitation to participate in the research and so we see no reason why this method should yield better results than any other which relies on self-selection.

Previous studies have also contacted men once they have entered the criminal justice system. Monto and Hotaling (2001), for example, administered a survey to 700 men who had been arrested for offences related to commercial sex. Faugier, Hayes and Butterworth (1992) identified their respondents via local police stations. An obvious limitation of this type of approach is that it only includes men that have been arrested for sex-related offences, which not only may be biased in itself, but may influence the kind of responses men give when questioned.

A further approach employed by a number of researchers is to advertise for volunteers to take part in research, either through the printed media (for example, Campbell, 1998; McKeganey and Barnard, 1996) or via radio (Gemme *et al.*, 1984). Whilst there is no doubt that this approach can yield samples of men, the self-selecting nature of these samples should lead us to treat any data which result with caution. First of all, at a general level, it seems reasonable to treat *any* sample obtained in this way with caution, whatever the population concerned. This method of sampling clearly has a place in social research but responding to such an advertisement requires time, effort and commitment. It is an active process, implying that those who do so have some interest in having their views heard. Whether this interest results from commitment to some cause, or from some more personal need, in most cases the resultant study group is likely to be atypical. In the case of the clients of sex workers, it seems even more reasonable to suppose that men who respond to such advertisements are not typical of the population of men who pay for sex. The fact that paying for sex is so discreditable an activity is alone enough to recommend caution, and suggest that, in general, men who pay for sex will not be inclined to identify themselves to strangers in response to advertisements. As we shall argue in later chapters, such a course of action not only exposes an individual to the risk of public exposure, but may also pose a threat to the maintenance of a 'creditable' self-identity.

A further approach is to utilise women who work in the sex industry to act as researchers and gather data on their clients (for example, see Kinnell, 1989). Whilst such an approach does not suffer so obviously from the biases inherent in the methods so far discussed, it is not without difficulties. First of all, there is the not insignificant difficulty of recruiting willing individuals and of equipping them with sufficient skills to undertake the investigations required – although these are not insurmountable and is, in fact, becoming a widely adopted method of social research. Secondly, there is the problem of perspective: just as clients have an interest in maintaining a particular self-identity, so do female sex workers. Data gathered in this way must therefore be considered as 'filtered' by the perspective and interests of the sex worker; what these might be will obviously vary but it seems likely that such women will have an interest – like their clients – in presenting themselves in as creditable a light as possible. Vanwesenbeeck *et al.*, (1993), for example, constructed a typology of men who pay for sex based on the accounts given by female sex workers. Wojcicki and Malala carried out interviews with 50 female sex workers in Johannesburg, South Africa, claiming that on the basis of this they were able to 'explore sexual negotiations between men and women in the sex industry' (2001, p.99). It is worth pausing here to reflect on the extent to which much of our knowledge and understanding of the men who pay for sex has been based on the accounts of female sex workers, rather than men themselves.

Recently, some other approaches have been documented. For example, Pitts *et al.*, (2004) sampled men at a large commercial event in Melbourne, Australia – the *Sexpo* exhibition – which offered products and services concerning all aspects of sex and sexuality. Clearly, the men attending such an event are less likely to be those who, for whatever reason, wish to conceal their interest in all things sexual. However, one of the advantages is that the researchers were able to reach over 600 men. There is also some evidence of increasing use of the internet as a form of data collection; for example, the use of internet surveys (see Atchison, Fraser and Lowman, 1998).

Men's Cyber-accounts of Paid-For-Sex

In conducting the present study, we have used a relatively novel approach to gathering data on men who pay for sex. We have not attempted to collect primary data from clients themselves, but have instead analysed a significant number of accounts, posted on the net, of men's encounters with sex workers. The remainder of this section is devoted to a description of how we collected and analysed our data. We then go on to discuss the various methodological issues which our approach raises.

PunterNet.com

Our data are drawn from a British website called *PunterNet* (www.PunterNet. com), the banner headline for which reads: 'The Online Community for Patrons and Providers of Adult Personal Services in the UK'. This website has been in existence since January 1999 and on its launch claimed the attention of leading newspapers, one of which described the site as, '... the most successful of the prostitute-reviewing internet sites' (London Evening Standard). The following is the site's own description of its aims:

> This site was created to facilitate the exchange of information on prostitution in the UK. Here you will find information on where to find services, what to expect, legalities, etc. You will be able to read reviews of encounters with working girls and submit your own 'field reports'. This web site aims to promote better understanding between customers and ladies in hopes that everyone may benefit, with less stressful, more enjoyable and mutually respectful visits (www.PunterNet.com).

The site is dedicated primarily to the publication of 'reviews' of encounters with female sex workers, although there are a number of other sections, including links to women's own websites; these are discussed in Chapter 3.

PunterNet is not unique, but has a number of characteristics which set it apart from other websites dealing with commercial sex. First is its longevity. At the time of writing it has existed, in a consistent format, for over seven years. Second, it does not appear to be primarily commercial in nature. Although *PunterNet* does carry links to a limited number of advertisements, its purpose, as illustrated in the quotation above, appears mainly to be, to provide information for men who use the services of female sex workers. In this sense it is unlike commercial sex websites, which exist primarily as a source of profit, and much more like the millions of websites which have been set up and run by enthusiasts for the benefit of fellow enthusiasts. It is not insignificant that the site refers to the practice of visiting sex workers as 'the hobby', the men who do so as 'hobbyists', and the reviews it publishes as 'field reports'. Frank's (2002) work on strip clubs is similar in that she reports how men view patronage of such clubs as a pastime or hobby – just a form of contemporary leisure. Indeed, the *PunterNet* host, who names himself *Galahad*, describes himself in the following way: 'I'm just a regular bloke, one of whose hobbies happens to be commercial sex'.

Another similarity to 'enthusiast' sites is the fact that *PunterNet* has an interactive message board facility. This appears to be widely used and, significantly, is used not only as a forum for the exchange of information between men but also for interaction between clients and women themselves. This has a number of implications. Firstly, we consider *PunterNet* to be a kind of 'virtual community' in which a set of norms, which to some extent are *contra* to prevailing social norms, can exist and guide discourse. Secondly, however, the presence of female sex workers as willing participants in this virtual community suggests their complicity in the manufacture and maintenance of these norms.

It is important to emphasise that *PunterNet* is concerned only with a specific kind of sex work. The site invites reviews of commercial (almost exclusively hetero) sex between consenting adults, and as we have outlined in Chapter 1, there are likely to be considerable differences between women working in different sectors of the industry. This book deals solely – as far as we are aware – with voluntary adult sex work (Scambler and Scambler, 1997). As O'Connell Davidson points out, the market for (hetero)sex work is widely segmented and the punters represented here are more likely to be 'better off and/or more cautious or inexperienced', in comparison to those who visit street prostitutes and are more likely to be looking for 'cheap "quickies"' (1996, p.182).

It is noteworthy that *PunterNet* and its contributors appear to endorse a set of moral boundaries about what is, and is not, acceptable in relation to issues of netiquette but also, of most interest to us, in the world of paid-for-sex. For example, the site seeks to set moral boundaries around talk on women in that it does not allow what it would define as derogatory talk, and rejects distasteful sexual activities (for example, any kind of 'shit play'). Most notably, however, the site carries an advertisement for *Crimestoppers* (a charity aimed at the prevention of crime in the UK) and invites anyone who has become aware of child prostitution to contact this organisation and report the details – it states: 'Have you been offered an underage girl? Report child prostitution – ring *Crimestoppers* on 0800 555 111'.

Data Collection

At the time of our analysis – carried out between 1999 and 2000 – *PunterNet* contained 5067 'reviews' (or 'field reports') of 2661 different women written by 2554 different authors. Whilst the majority of authors post just one field report, many published several, the highest number for any one individual being 46. Similarly whilst the majority of women are reviewed only once, many are reviewed several times, the highest number being 32. We chose to sample the reviews by author and, at random, selected a 10 per cent sample (n=255). Since several of these authors had published more than one field report, we randomly selected one of their reports to be included in the sample. At the time of writing, there were 33,979 field reports written by 17,040 authors. The highest number of posts by any author was 94 and the highest number of posts for an individual woman was 147.

The field reports are highly structured. When posting a report, authors must complete an on-line pro-forma, which gives details of the woman's name, the location of the encounter (town and, in some cases, actual address), telephone number and/or website address, price paid, and length of time taken. Comments are then organized under three headings: 'her place', 'description' and 'comments'. Finally, punters are asked to indicate whether they would recommend her to others and whether they would visit her again themselves; as expected, the reviews vary quite considerably in length and level of detail. To give you a flavour of these field reports in their entirety, we have included a fairly typical field report below:

Field Report on 'Shannon' of Coalville

Posted:	February 29, 2000
From:	A. Mouse 'nonny'
Day of Week:	Sun
Time of Day:	2.20pm
Location:	Coalville
Lady Advertises By:	Online
Contact:	01530817090
Time:	50min
Price:	£40
Her Place:	On High Street above shops, opposite Ford Garage. Sauna & shower facilities
Description:	Dark hair, tanned olive skin. Early 30's but in very good condition. Very slim figure but busty, 36B/C
Comments:	Very nice gentle massage, back and front, then reeled off 'menu': R £25, + rev mass £40, VIP sex £50, Anal £80.

Opted for reverse massage. I began massaging her, very slim, not an ounce of fat. Started on her back then began fingering her pussy. Did this for ages. She seemed to enjoy it. Turned over, continued my attention to her nicely shaven pussy. Munched away for a while till my jaw started to ache, she responded with erotic moaning. Then played with her breasts – nice responsive nipples – before going down on her one last brief time while she fondled her tits and pushed my mouth down hard on her clit.

She then started wanking me as I came back up for a second go at her firm breasts. Held on for as long as I could before spraying her breasts with large amounts of hot cum. She continued wanking me & pressing my helmet against her still-hard nips.

Wow is all I can say. The best I've ever had – particularly liked the muff-diving. My knees were still shaking an hour later. Warmly recommended.

Would You Return:	Yes.

Data Analysis

Our analysis of the data is based on an iterative process of reading and rereading the field reports. Some analysis was completed manually using traditional methods of pen and paper, initially highlighting what seemed to be important words or passages with a marker pen. We did not embark on our analysis with a particular set of categories or themes but attempted to allow these to 'emerge' from the process of reading and rereading men's accounts. We are not suggesting an entirely inductive approach to our data analysis, since we do not believe that this is possible, but we have attempted to ground our analysis in what men have to say about their experiences of paying for sex.

Once the data had been preliminarily analysed for the purpose of identifying important words or passages, we then began to explore some of the issues and concepts that emerged from this, mindful of the already existing literature on the sex industry. For example, we were intrigued to discover men writing about girlfriend sex, or the 'girlfriend experience', which prompted us to consider issues of intimacy, amongst others. Using pen and paper we then annotated the data in the margins and made additional separate research notes.

Although the data were predominantly analysed manually, we did then import the data into the Computer Assisted Qualitative Data Analysis Software program *N.Vivo*. We adopted this approach for purely pragmatic reasons in that such software can perform traditional tasks more swiftly. As Coffey, Holbrook and Atkins state:

> The speed and comprehensiveness of searches is an undoubted benefit: the computer does not search the data file until it comes up with the first example that will 'do' to illustrate an argument, nor will it stop after it has found just one or a couple of apposite quotes or vignettes. The software has an additional merit that definitely marks an advance on the practical value of manual coding and searching: it can cope with multiple and overlapping codes; it can conduct multiple searches, using more than one codeword simultaneously (Coffey, Holbrook and Atkins, 1996, para. 7.2).

We used *N.Vivo* to search for and retrieve data, as well as to code and retrieve data in the manner described above. However, by using data that have been written by others and posted on the net, searching for particular words and phrases could be difficult given the range of spelling and typographical errors present in the material, and this presented an additional challenge when using a software program. Also, in spite of the oft claimed advantages of using computer analysis software, and the many complex tasks they claim to perform we, like many others, did not make use of these, as Kelle notes:

> ... in practice, many users of computer software restrict themselves to ordinary coding and retrieval and do not exploit the various possibilities of 'third generation' or 'theory building' software (Kelle, 1997, para. 2.9).

There has been considerable debate on the use of qualitative software programs and their role in data analysis. It has been argued that many researchers purport to use such functions in an attempt to claim increased rigour against the critique that qualitative research is intuitive, rather than systematic (Lee and Fielding, 1995); 'arguments of that kind seem to be often used by others as a strategic means to convince funding boards that the proposed research endeavour will be carried out in a rigorous and scholarly way' (Kelle, 1997, para 1.4).

Whilst qualitative analysis can be transparent, it is necessarily interpretive and intuitive and we have essentially used computer software as a tool for archiving and data administration rather than as a tool for data analysis. Whilst computers can be useful in this respect we dislike the way in which they can seem to remove the researcher from a seemingly physical proximity to the data. Software analysis also means that data analysis can only really take place at a computer, thus limiting physical freedom.

Another issue that we consider here is that of interpretation and understanding of data. This is, of course, not limited solely to data obtained from the net, but applies equally to all written forms of communication. Some researchers have argued that by relying on written information, the nuances of face-to-face communication are lost, thus leading to less rich, and less valid, data. For example, Illingworth (2001, para. 14.3) explains: 'The lack of physicality and reliance on written rather than verbal communication potentially leads to the loss of important observational elements and cues vital to the validation of researcher-respondent exchange', for example, sighs. Whilst such observations cannot be made in internet mediated research, this is not to say that other cues do not exist. Men's accounts on *PunterNet* demonstrate that many observations can be made about the way in which men write and the methods by which they highlight their points of view. For example, exclamation marks are often used for emphasis:

> ... really enjoyed myself, if your paying for it, you might as well have the best, and trust me this lady is!!!!! [Bigfoot, #24]

> Worth anyone's time to visit – if you're not delighted you must be dead!!!!! [Davy, #56]

As is capitalisation:

> YES, she likes you to have a shower first (and YES there is a jokey sign about the wet towels). [Dave Browne, #42]

> ... was dying to meet her, and was more than pleased with what i saw. in a nutshell – WOW! [Elephantman, #68]

The use of inverted commas is also evident as a means of expressing irony or when employing one of the commonly used dictums which are part of the normative world of *PunterNet*. For example:

Suffice to say, "treat this lovely lady right, and you won't be disappointed". [Altosax, #8]

she prefers the longer appointments to get to know people ... rather than the 2hour "wham bam thank u mam" appointment. [David Murphy, #55]

So, whilst we are not arguing that internet-mediated research is identical to research that is carried out face-to-face, there are clear textual observations that can be made, adding richness to our interpretation and understanding.

Authenticity of Cyber-Accounts

A fairly obvious question which our approach raises is the extent to which data collected in this way can be considered 'authentic'. Indeed, one of the first questions we asked ourselves when we stumbled across this site was: is this for real? There are in fact a number of dimensions to this question which, to a very considerable extent, is raised equally by any first-person account. Writing generally about the use of life documents, Jones suggests that the following should be considered:

Authenticity:	Does the document cohere and make sense? Is it unique, a reliable source, and consistent?
Credibility:	Who produced it? Why, when, for whom, and in what context was it produced?
Representativeness:	Is it reasonable to assume that the document is a typical example from the universe of similar documents?
Meaning:	Does the document have a surface meaning? Does it have an underlying, deeper meaning that we can acquire through some form of interpretative understanding ... (Jones, 2000, p.559)

Perhaps the most obvious dimension to the question of authenticity is the extent to which we can be confident that the accounts are indeed written by genuine clients, in the light of a genuine encounter with a sex worker. In cyberspace, individuals can represent themselves as anyone they please, changing their age or gender – and in places such as multi-user domains – they can become entirely fantastic (Turkle, 1995). Even with other forms of net use, such as participation in *PunterNet*, it is possible that individuals may offer a filtered representation of themselves and reality. However, in contrast to earlier thought, there is now a growing body of opinion suggesting that the presentation of self in 'real life' and on the net may be fairly convergent (Mann and Stewart, 2000). And, indeed, that individuals may be more likely to represent themselves and their actions honestly on the net in comparison to more traditional forms of face-to-face communication or research. The advantage of this idea, as Illingworth (2001) suggests, is that this perspective allows us to consider the extent to which on and offline experiences may be connected and may influence one another.

Can we rule out, though, the possibility that accounts are purely fictional, or written by someone – a sex worker, perhaps – in an attempt to boost business? As Poster suggests in his discussion of narratives in cyberspace:

> Individuals appear to enjoy relating narratives to those they have never met and probably never will meet. These narratives often seem to emerge directly from people's lives but many no doubt are inventions (Poster, 1995, p.91).

Whilst it is obviously impossible to rule these things out altogether, there are a number of reasons why we are entitled to treat these possibilities with scepticism. First of all, there is the sheer volume of 'field reports'. Whilst some accounts may be fantastic, it seems most unlikely that the many thousands of individuals who post on the *PunterNet* site will all be deliberately posting false or purely fictional accounts. However, Jordan – writing about the politics and culture of cyberspace – argues that cyberspace interactions are 'riven by competitive and sometimes abusive forms of communication' (2001, p.6). He identifies the action of 'trolling', which he describes as the deliberate posting of a false message to see if someone will take it seriously and reply. Indeed, not all field reports will appear on the site if *Galahad*, the website host, believes the report to be deliberately false or malicious. Of course, it is not impossible that there might be a few individuals sufficiently motivated to write and post purely fictional accounts.

Secondly, and reinforcing this, many of the accounts are very brief, or otherwise lacking in detail, and this hardly seems consistent with their being fictional products of fantasy, where one would anticipate much longer, more detailed and salacious accounts of paying for sex. Thirdly, there are sufficient external references contained within the reports – such as telephone numbers, websites and addresses – to suggest that the basis of the vast majority of the reports was a genuine sexual encounter. Indeed, more anecdotally, we also know that sex workers themselves chat about *PunterNet* and discuss how they have been reviewed on the site. Many independent escorts also provide links to *PunterNet* field reports on their websites. Finally, most reports adopt a tone which is critical and evaluative. A small number are overtly critical or hostile, but many more contain what appear to be balanced judgements, mentioning both positive and negative features of the encounter or the woman concerned. This suggests that it is unlikely that many have been written by or on behalf of the woman in question.

A further dimension to the question of authenticity is the difficult issue of how far the account given can be considered a 'true' or 'valid' reflection of the events which actually took place. This question is of course not peculiar to accounts published on the net, but is raised by any attempt to employ first-hand accounts as a source of data. For, example, Plummer, writing about the use of autobiography and life history research states:

> It does not matter if the account can later be shown to be false in particulars – most accounts, even so-called 'scientific' ones, are context bound and speak to certain people,

times and circumstances. What matters, therefore in life history research is the facilitation of as full a subjective view as possible (1983, pp.14-15).

Most obviously, men giving accounts could deliberately ignore certain salient features of the encounter or, equally, embellish their accounts with invented detail. More subtly, accounts will reflect, perhaps in quite unconscious ways, the particular standpoint of the individual writing the account. An important aspect of this is the motivation which lies behind the act of 'giving an account'.

Account giving is motivated by interests: a statement made to police about one's alleged involvement in a crime is likely to be motivated by the very obvious interest of remaining at large. An account given to one's spouse, after an unplanned meeting with a lover will be motivated by a desire for concealment. An account given to a child, about why a parent cannot attend his or her birthday party, will be motivated by a desire to present oneself as a loving parent, and to counter what the child perceives as evidence to the contrary. Such interests may result in accounts which are straightforwardly dissimulated – the thief who claims to have been nowhere near the scene of the crime, for example. More routinely – and arguably always – such accounts will be selective; they will dwell on certain features of the events which are salient for the interests being served, and overlook others which threaten to undermine the 'case' of the account-giver. It follows that any attempt to interpret an account, must take into consideration the interests and standpoint of the account-giver. In day-to-day interaction this occurs routinely, whether it is a police officer interpreting the account of a criminal suspect, or a suspicious wife questioning her husband's account of an unexplained absence. Exactly the same principle applies to the researcher interrogating accounts given by the researched, in our case, men who give accounts of their experiences with female sex workers. These accounts offer an opportunity to examine the way in which men who pay for sex manage deviant sexual identities through the construction of sexual stories. Plummer describes sexual stories as 'narratives of the intimate' arguing that 'there is no point in telling a tale without a receptive and appreciative listener, and one who is usually part of a wider community of support' (1996, pp.34-5). Stories have been described as the bases of identity or as 'narrative truths' (Spence, 1982; Bruner, 1987). Men's stories of commercial sex have long-since been muted and relegated to the inner world of telling stories to the self and have seldom been shared so publicly until now.

We must, therefore, pose the question: what interests are being served by the act of writing an account of a commercial sexual experience and publishing this account anonymously on a website dedicated to publishing such accounts? On the face of it, this is a difficult question to answer. As we have already noted, paying for sex is a potentially discrediting act and, depending upon the man's social and marital status, one whose revelation could have catastrophic consequences. In most conceivable cases, concealment would have to be the goal of any account relating to such activity (for example, in explaining one's absence from home or work, or one's presence in a questionable part of town or the withdrawal of unexplained sums of money from one's bank account). Superficially, there seems to be no incentive whatsoever to reveal anything about such activity to anyone, let alone to take the trouble to publish what are often lengthy and highly revealing accounts on the net! This is even more surprising when we remember that many of the accounts include an email address for the author. Thus even if such email accounts are generally private, the possibility exists that any reader of the account could respond directly to the author and solicit interaction on the subject of the account.

In spite of these preliminary observations, however, we contend that there are some very real interests being served by the act of publishing accounts of sexual activity with sex workers on the net. Furthermore, our grasp of these interests is the key to interpreting the accounts, and to arriving at a satisfactory conclusion to the question of 'authenticity'.

The Normative World of *PunterNet.com*

In writing reviews for *PunterNet* we suggest that men are 'performing' masculinity against a backdrop of a particular normative order which allows them to maintain a creditable heterosexual masculine identity, whilst acknowledging that they pay for sex. An understanding of this normative order is essential, therefore, in any attempt to interpret these accounts. Whilst any attempt to describe something as abstract and embracing as a 'normative order' is bound to be highly partial, we have set out below what seem to us to be they key features of the particular normative order which defines the *PunterNet* community.

Paying for sex, per se, raises no moral issues Nowhere in the data did we find any reference to any of the moral debates which, in the wider community, surround paying for sex. The absence of any references to such debates suggests a normative order in which the legitimacy of such questions is simply not acknowledged, rather than one in which certain well-considered positions are adopted. The fact that writers clearly feel no need to justify their actions against hostile moral positions (which would almost certainly be the case if they discussed their actions in the wider community) suggests a moral world in which such debates have simply been bracketed out.

That is not to say, however, that there are no clear moral boundaries which define this community. It is clearly assumed that commercial sex with underage girls is morally unacceptable, as is the failure of a punter to pay a legitimate fee for services provided. Violence against women is also clearly morally proscribed. Equally, however, there are practices engaged in by some sex workers which are considered to transgress moral boundaries, and these include taking the money but not providing the service and mis-representation of appearance, price or services offered. Links are provided to websites which offer information exchange on problem punters or sex workers and various women's advice groups which provide support for victims of sex trafficking and violence, for example, www.escortwatch.co.uk.

Explicit accounts of intimate sexual acts are legitimate and necessary Most accounts in our data set contain highly explicit accounts of intimate sexual acts. These accounts employ sexually explicit language and graphically describe instances of oral sex, masturbation, anal and vaginal intercourse and ejaculation. Whilst humour is not altogether absent in the accounts, they are in general straightforwardly descriptive and words such as 'cock', 'pussy', 'cunt', 'tits', 'cum', 'fuck', 'wank' etc., are generally used without irony or humour or, strangely, erotic intent. The use of such language in a purely descriptive mode sets apart the world of *PunterNet* from both mainstream morality (where such words are taboo), and the culture of the male locker-room (where such terms are used, but with humour or irony) (see, for example, Kehily and Nayak, 1997).

Paying for sex is 'normal' An overwhelming feature of the normative world of *PunterNet* is that paying for sex is normal, routine and wholly compatible with a regular heterosexual masculine identity. A prevailing assumption seems to be that there is nothing out of the ordinary about paying for sex. The term 'hobby' is used regularly to describe the practice, which seems to locate paying for sex firmly in the category of an innocuous pastime (such as playing golf or collecting stamps) rather than as a deviant and dangerous sexual practice, which is how society in general more commonly regards it.

The vast majority of reviewers are 'regulars' and make detailed and sometimes fine distinctions between experiences. The language employed often verges on that of the connoisseur, revealing (or claiming) considerable experience and mature tastes. In the same way that it would be most unusual to find connoisseurs of fine wine debating the underlying morality or wisdom of consuming alcohol, one does not find the authors on *PunterNet* debating the essential morality or wisdom of paying for sex.

One of the most crucial of the underlying assumptions of *PunterNet's* normative world (and one explored further in later chapters) is that paying for sex does *not* imply that the punter is incapable of obtaining voluntary sexual partners. The act of paying for sex does not imply any lack of sexual attractiveness or sexual inadequacy of any kind. The act of punting seems somehow to lie outside of the man's normal sexual relationships and is largely irrelevant to them.

The woman is a 'lady' Whilst, as we shall explore throughout this book, men's perceptions of female sex workers are complex and often contradictory, there is an underlying assumption that they are professionals and, thus, worthy of respect. That is not to say that one does not find seemingly offensive remarks amongst the reviews, but these are invariably 'justified' by some failure of the woman concerned to provide an adequate, or *professional*, level of service. The default attitude seems to be one in which sex workers are essentially good, decent women who work hard to provide a high level of service. Men's perceptions thus echo the increasingly held view that sex work is ordinary work. In this respect the assumption is quite different from prevailing attitudes towards sex workers in wider society; they are seen neither as 'victims' nor as moral outcasts.

Awareness of the two distinct normative worlds Whilst we argue that in important respects *PunterNet* constitutes a distinct normative world, that is not to say that the men who contribute reviews are in any sense unaware of or uninfluenced by the wider normative world which they inhabit. We are not proposing a distinct 'sub-culture', but rather a (virtual) space in which certain specific common normative assumptions are suspended and modified in such a way as makes participation in a deviant sexual activity morally and psychologically easier than if practised in social isolation. The fact that men are concerned about being seen entering the premises of a sex worker (see Chapter 7) or about being exposed as punters to their wives, girlfriends and workmates clearly demonstrates their overall commitment to mainstream values.

What all of this means for the interpretation of our data is that, in writing reviews for *PunterNet*, men are entering and contributing to a normative world in which paying for sex has none of the morality threatening, or identity-threatening features which it does in the context of wider society. We therefore suggest that writing reviews of paying for sex has the effect of *neutralising* a significant threat to personal identity, a threat posed inevitably by the act of paying for sex. An appreciation that this interest is being served when a man writes a review has been central to our interpretation of the data and the analysis we have developed.

Ethical Issues in the Research

All research raises ethical questions. The ethical guidelines outlined by the British Sociological Association, for example, make clear that issues of consent are paramount when conducting research:

> As far as possible participation in sociological research should be based on the freely given informed consent of those studied. This implies a responsibility on the sociologist to explain in appropriate detail, and in terms meaningful to participants, what the research is about, who is undertaking and financing it, why it is being undertaken, and how it is to be disseminated and used ... Research participants should be made aware of their right to refuse participation whenever and for whatever reason they wish (http://www.britsoc. co.uk).

However, internet mediated research (IMR) raises specific questions concerning the maintenance of ethical standards. Hewson *et al.*, argue that:

> The problem ... is not so much that adequate ethical procedures cannot be ensured in IMR, as the lack of a set of clear and widely accepted guidelines outlining appropriate and effective procedures ... [which] are just beginning to be identified and addressed (Hewson *et al.*, 2003, p.51).

And on the subject of covert study, the British Sociological Association state:

There are serious ethical and legal issues in the use of covert research but the use of covert methods may be justified in certain circumstances ... covert methods violate the principles of informed consent and may invade the privacy of those being studied (http://www.britsoc.co.uk).

A number of specific ethical issues are raised by the method we have used in this study. The most general of these relates to the status of the material we have used, and the extent to which it is ethically legitimate to use it as a source of data. In our view this issue arises from the fact that the material was not intended as data to be used by social scientists, rather than anything to with the fact that the material was posted on the net. The same issue is raised, for example, by social scientists or historians who use personal diaries or other documents as a source of data: material is produced for one purpose and then appropriated by social scientists for another without the knowledge or consent of the author. It seems to us that such concerns are mitigated by three main factors: firstly, whether or not the material was placed in the public domain by its author; secondly, whether any deception was required to access the material and thirdly, whether the use of the material by social scientists in any way harms or compromises the authors or subjects of the material.

If we take the first of these mitigating factors, it is clear that the material we have used was placed in the public domain by its authors. It is worth noting, however, that whether or not something is placed in the public domain is not always clear-cut in the case of internet research. Hine and Eve (1998), for example, have argued that the question of privacy on the net is complex, and that there is a case for considering the concept of 'situated privacy'; referring to the way in which researchers reflect on the purpose of the website and the rules of those who use it. Humphreys (1970) work on the tea-room trade, for example, exposed the private interactions of men who had sex with other men in public toilets. This research would now be ethically questionable and maybe so, too, is ours.

On the net 'the public domain' is best seen as a continuum ranging from the strictly private and protected (such as personal bank account details) through to sites which are completely open to anyone who has internet access. In between there are various shades of openness, from sites that require a password to enter, where passwords are readily issued to anyone who asks for or pays for one, to sites which are restricted to members of particular organisations or who claim some special characteristic required for access. *PunterNet* falls into the category of the most publicly accessible kind of website: anyone can anonymously access and read any material posted on the site. Fox and Roberts (1999) suggest that researchers must be mindful of the difference between internet data that is 'publicly accessible' and that which is 'publicly disseminated'. Whilst the *PunterNet* data probably fall into the former category we feel that the use of such data is still permissible. As Soothill and Sanders (2005) have rightly noted, the openly accessible status of the website and of all the information posted on it is often acknowledged on the *PunterNet* site itself, with the expectation that researchers, journalists, the police and others, will be frequent 'lurkers'.

We have been frequent lurkers on this site for many years, and since *PunterNet* is a publicly open site no deception was necessary to access the material. However, the issue of harm or compromise is a little more complex. Although the reviews can be anonymous, many appear with a seemingly valid email address at their head. Reviewers select a name by which they will be known, and we have retained these names in our presentation of the data, although we have not revealed any email addresses. Whilst it is conceivable that individuals could be identified by these chosen names, our view is that because individuals have chosen to publish reviews in a public forum under these names, we are not significantly increasing their risk of exposure by retaining them in the study. Nevertheless, we should acknowledge at least a theoretical chance that an individual who has chosen a name by which they can easily be identified might come to the attention of a significantly different audience through our publication of this study, than by simply posting a review on *PunterNet*. Fairly early on in the study we rejected the idea of contacting authors via their email addresses on ethical grounds. Whilst it would certainly have been interesting to have made direct contact with authors, and to have sought data on their backgrounds and experiences of paying for sex, we felt that the danger of our email approach being apprehended by someone other than the author was too great. As with any ethnographic study, we have abided by the rules of the group that has been studied, and have tried not to put individuals in a position that could cause them any harm.

The Implications of Sex in Cyberspace

The remit of our research largely extends to an exploration of men's cyber-accounts of commercial sex; our interests lie, in the most part, in understanding the representation, performance and construction of heterosexual masculine identities. As we have discussed in Chapter 1, our research follows in the sociological tradition of research which seeks to explore and understand sexual deviance, rather than change it, or make things 'better'. However, many would argue that social scientists should not really carry out research without, at least, considering the wider implications for the 'real world' and, of course, better understanding may subsequently influence change. As such, the implications of sex in cyberspace may well have wider ethical and moral implications that those we have been able to discuss here. For example, it may have implications for the surveillance of HIV and sexually transmitted infections and the wider public health agenda. We seek to address some of these concerns within Chapter 7, by revisiting the epistemological tensions raised by our method.

The net has offered sociologists, and others, information to which they have not previously had access. It presents enormous and exciting possibilities and the opportunity to research hard-to-reach populations or to research issues of a sensitive nature. We agree with Jones (1999) who argues that the net has provided us with a 'seductive data set'. However, other researchers have urged caution, for example:

... the temptation to see the development of this collection of new research techniques as providing an easily accessible route to previously hidden populations must be countered (Illingworth, 2001, para. 1.1).

It is worth noting, of course, that just as other methods of data collection are inherently biased, research on the net is restricted to those who can and do use the internet. Whilst *PunterNet* includes reviews which relate to different forms of indoor sex work, it is restricted to reviews posted by men who have (probably private) access to computers. Whilst, for our purposes, this is not necessarily problematic, it is significant in terms of men's background, education and resources and may be pertinent to the wider implications of our research.

A Footnote on Method

Since men who pay for sex and post their accounts on *PunterNet* are most likely already using pseudonyms, we have used the names that men themselves have given as a means of identifying quotations. Even if pseudonyms have not been used, and we cannot be sure either way, we have identified quotations by the names given on the site. A study of nicknames on the net (Bechar-Israeli, 1995) suggested that about eight per cent of users will probably use their real names, approximately 45 per cent will choose a nickname that says something about them in some way, and only six per cent will choose an entirely fanciful name. Whilst we do not dwell on these especially, it is interesting to note some of the names used on *PunterNet* here: for example, *Tommo*, *Wandering Willy*, *Ugly Bastard*, *Zx-9*, and *Michael*. When men write about their experiences they refer to specific women and places and this must be considered too. Given the increasing use of the internet to advertise commercial sex and that fact that *PunterNet* is a public site (as we have already discussed at length above) we feel justified in using the names and places given within the site. We can also be fairly sure that sex workers use pseudonyms and that, by using the names by which men have referred to them, that we are unlikely to reveal their true identities. For example, Sanders' (2005) study of sex workers in Birmingham revealed that of the 55 women she interviewed, only 3 used their birth names. The others used a pseudonym – a proper name or feminine word – which (like the pseudonyms adopted by men) were usually allusive and sexually suggestive. As Sanders notes: 'In the sex industry, the pseudonym, like other trade names, is used freely and openly advertised in newspapers and on websites' (2005, p.124).

As with many written accounts on the net, we found considerable spelling, and typographical, errors within men's accounts. To avoid altering meaning and to prevent concealing some important features of men's stories we have generally quoted men verbatim. Where spelling or typographical errors substantially hindered meaning we have corrected the text. Where other words or phrases have been incorporated into the text, this is represented by: [-].

Chapter 3

Bodies for Hire

Sex, Bodies and Commodities

The purpose of this chapter is to explore the commodification and objectification of women's bodies in relation to *PunterNet*, and the internet more generally. We begin by focusing on sex workers and, specifically, on the ways in which they have utilized internet technology to represent and promote their services. We consider, first of all, the ways in which the internet has been used by providers of sexual services as a 'shop window'. Within this we reflect, also, on the ways in which this technology has allowed 'service providers' to construct and represent sex work in particular ways; ways, we argue, which constitute a significant departure from those of the pre-cyberspace era. We then turn to men's accounts and explore their representations of women's bodies. We analyse their narratives and consider the significance of representation and authenticity. Central to an analysis of women's bodies for hire is the concept that Blanchard (1994) calls 'McSex', reflecting the concept of sex as a commodity rather than as part of consensual non-commercial relationship. According to one of the men interviewed by Blanchard for her article in the magazine *Mademoiselle*, sex is 'like going to McDonalds; most of the people are looking for a good, fast meal at a good price. It's satisfying, it's fattening, and after, you get out of there quickly' (Blanchard, 1994, p.80).

Selling Sex on the Net

Any cursory internet search will reveal a huge number of sites dedicated to advertising the services of escorts, call girls, masseuses, and so on. Such sites take a number of forms, but seem to centre on several distinct types. Firstly, there are the agency sites. These tend to be highly professional in their design, and are run by agencies which manage anywhere between two or three and a hundred women. Some are organized by geographical location and some by type of women specialized in. We have found, for example, agencies dedicated exclusively to 'Asian', 'oriental', 'Black' and 'large-breasted' women, and others where it is possible to search by these or other characteristics (for example, hair colour and age group). In general, agency sites display a common pricing structure and terms and conditions, although individual women may vary in the services which they offer. It is often possible to search by service provision – for example, for women who will rim, French kiss, do anal, entertain couples, and so on. Generally, contact is made via the agency either by telephone or, more commonly, email. It is not uncommon to find agency sites which advertise credit card facilities, and some require credit card payment or deposits in advance of the encounter. In general, agencies advertise higher prices than other categories, presumably in order to recover an overhead.

Secondly, there are sites which advertise independent escorts. These are much more variable in nature. Many are highly professional, similar to most agency sites, whilst others are much more amateurish. There are also a number of sites which host independent escorts' pages; these are often similar in format to agency sites, although much more variation in pricing, terms and conditions and services provided is usually evident. In the case of independents, contact is generally made with the woman directly, again either by email or telephone. Some independents offer specially discounted rates for regular punters and, as we have already highlighted in Chapter 2, there are often links to the *PunterNet* field reports. It is made very clear on each website that payment is for time and companionship only.

Thirdly, there are sites associated with massage parlours. These tend to vary quite considerably in nature, but will usually give details of women who are employed there, location, opening times and facilities provided. Information and pricing will also be given on the range of 'massages' available. For example, a parlour in England (East Midlands) offers the following:

Half hour full body massage	£25
Half hour tie and tease massage	£50
Half hour lap dance massage	£50
Three quarter all in massage	£75
One hour double bubble massage	£85

Whatever the detailed differences between the ways in which the various categories of provider represent themselves on the net, there are certain features which they virtually all have in common. Almost all providers, whatever their category, include photographs of the women on their websites. The majority include professional or near professional standard glamour shots, varying from one or two to several albums of a dozen images or more. Poses are rarely of an explicit hardcore nature, but usually involve provocative clothing (for example, scanty lingerie, stockings and suspenders, basques and g-strings) and many include semi-nude poses – most commonly, exposed breasts and thighs. The overwhelming majority of images clearly seek to replicate the style of top-shelf pornography. As Sanders argues, sex workers manufacture their identities in such a way as to 'manipulate the cultural ideals of sexualized femininity to attract and maintain custom and make financial gain' (2005, p.143). Whilst many sites include full facial photographs of the women – a fair number do not. Where this is explained, it is generally in terms of the need for discretion on the part of the woman herself. Those sites least likely to include photographs are those of massage parlours; sometimes they do not include any shots, but most commonly they include only partial coverage of the entire staff. The most likely explanation for this is staff turnover.

The vast majority of sites also include a statement of pricing. With escorts – either agency or independent – pricing is usually by the hour. Some offer half hourly appointments and most give a price list ranging from an hour to a week. Modest discounts are usually built into multiples of hour long appointments. In some cases, prices are listed by sex act – oral sex, vaginal sex, anal sex and so on. It is not common to see the details of these prices on websites, but where individual pricing is applied some reference is usually made to this.

Most sites contain a statement of what is and is not acceptable, or desirable, to each sex worker. These statements can vary from a list of sexual practices which women allegedly enjoy, to those which are essentially a list of prohibitions, for example, 'Kate's' site states:

> Just to put you in the picture at this early stage, the 'Services' I offer along with the full girlfriend experience are OWO and kissing. I do not however offer CIM or A. Personal hygiene is important to me and I would expect the same of you – naturally.

A slightly different approach is taken by 'Sindy':

> I really do prefer a full GFE (Girlfriend Experience), unrushed with plenty of kisses caresses and cuddling. My sexual favourites are 69, spanking, sex toys, mild domination, facials, French kissing, oral without (at discretion), voyeurism, giving watersports and receiving rimming.

Whilst on the face of it this appears to be an enticing list of sexual preferences, it also contains some clear limits to what the sex worker is prepared to do. In Sindy's case, giving watersports clearly implies that 'receiving' is off the agenda, whilst the converse seems to be true of rimming.

It is also clear, however, that sex workers operating at the higher end of the market advertise the pleasure which they themselves may potentially gain from engaging in sex with a client (see, also, Chapter 5). The extract below, taken from 'Paige's' website, shows her actively dealing with the potential anomaly of a sex worker receiving genuine pleasure from a sexual encounter for which she is paid:

> I am full of passion and I am willing to have fun and provide a great girlfriend experience. Just because you are paying for my time, it doesn't mean that we can't build up a friendship and that we should think any less of each other for it! I love my 'work' and it's the wonderful men I meet that make me feel that way.

In the same way, we find many examples of women actively marketing their personalities though their websites. 'Fun-loving', 'bubbly', 'charming' and 'intelligent' are descriptions given by women again and again. It seems, then, that the websites serve two distinct functions. One is to set the parameters of the potential encounter: details of price, location, terms and services available and proscribed. The second is to advertise the characteristics which are most likely to attract potential clients: appearance and bodily characteristics, personality and a liking for certain sexual activities.

The Objectification of Women's Bodies

There is a considerable amount of writing on women's bodies and the way that they are represented within popular culture. Feminist writing, in particular, has been critical of the way in which women's bodies are represented as the passive objects of male desire – especially within pornography (for example, see Dworkin, 1981). Many have argued that women are objectified in all cultural representations. For example, Berger argues that, 'Men act and women appear. Men look at women. Women watch themselves being looked at' (1972, p.47). This is the 'male gaze' – the voyeuristic consumption of women's bodies by men. Others such as Smith (1999) have argued that the representation of women's bodies is not as monolithic as previous analyses have suggested, arguing that there is scope for both resistance and transgression. Whether men visit a walk-up or massage parlour, or whether they arrange to visit an escort, their decision is often made through this gaze and the way in which women are represented on the net. Sullivan has argued: 'With the advent of the World Wide Web, women's objectification and its internalisation continue...' (1997, p.192). Of course, others would suggest that the opposite is true and have argued that net has the potential to transform sexualized gender relations.

On *PunterNet* men are asked to give a physical description of the sex worker they have visited within each of their field reports; a specific entry entitled 'Description' requires this. Attributes commonly referred to within this section include, age and ethnicity, her 'vital statistics', skin, hair and teeth, and descriptions of the woman's breasts, vagina, buttocks, and so on. The field reports indicate that men make aesthetic judgements based on normative cultural expectations and desires relating contemporary standards of female beauty (Bordo, 1993). Typical descriptions include:

> Mellissa is in her mid thirties, tanned with frizzy blonde hair and shaven. Average looking for her age. Breasts not as firm as i like them – OK I'm being overly fusssy. [Kerravon, #126]

No aspect of physical appearance is too small or too inconsequential to describe, for example:

> She is young, fun and considerate. Her breasts are small yet firm. Her legs are slim and nicely shaped. Her arse is just stunning. She does have discoloured teeth – but then, so do I... [Entranced, #60]

What follows below is an analysis of men's representations of women's bodies organized around specific core themes. Firstly, we consider the importance of authenticity and the problem of mis-selling. Then we explore fit, maternal, exotic and ageing bodies.

Authenticity and Representation

Representations of sex work, whether on the net or not, enable women and others to sell sex. However, these representations provide the vehicle for both buying and selling and, as such, issues of representation, as well as misrepresentation, must be considered. At a very general level, misrepresentation is problematic because it amounts to the problem of false advertising in which goods (women) and services (sex acts) are being mis-sold. Sex workers can falsely advertise by claiming to be younger or slimmer than they actually are, displaying photographs of someone other than themselves, or by claiming to provide services which are later prohibited. All of these, as we have outlined above, are important features of selling sex on the net. On *PunterNet*, men's accounts demonstrate an awareness of misrepresentation and having been mis-sold. Sometimes their accounts also serve to warn others of this practice:

> This girl is absolutely stunning. She was described by the receptionist as a leggy 19 year old blonde with waist length blonde hair and 34D bust (we've all heard that before haven't we). But this description is actually true! Angel is a genuine teenage bombshell. [Westman 41, #248]

> There are only ever two girls working at anyone time. Call the receptionist and she will give you a description of both, but be very careful, as she is apt to bullshit. [Wavygravy, #227]

Misrepresentation is also problematic because authentic representation is central to men's buying patterns and the fact that punters make choices based on how women are represented. On *PunterNet*, one man stated:

> This lady is a beauty, fancied her from the web site photo's – I wasn't disappointed, mid twenties, gorgeous long brunette hair, fantastic proportioned all over tanned body (38C 2636). Attractive smile and stunning blue eyes. [Richy, #201]

Campbell's (1998) study of men who pay for sex in Liverpool indicates that one of the reasons men pay for sex is because they can engage in sexual contact with women with particular physical characteristics. For example, one of Campbell's respondents state: 'There's some lovely women. I like to choose women who've got big breasts and an attractive figure' (1998, p.165). This is what Blanchard (1994) describes as McSex, illustrating how men shop for a sexual partner with specific bodily attributes, body type or hair colour. By expressing their likes and dislikes, men's accounts also show that they shop for women with particular attributes, for example:

> Charise is beautiful. No other way to describe her. If, like me, you like slim, petite and good looking girls, then Charise is for you. [Entranced, #69]

> Nice rounded figure, Not a hint of fat, but not skinny either. If you like large natural breasts Tyler would be an excellent choice! [Xizzy, #242]

Many accounts show men's dissatisfaction when women are represented in a way that is untrue or otherwise exaggerated, for example:

approx 45/50 nice face pleasant to look at normal size 12 not heavy NOT busty as advertised. [janothing, #108]

Advertised as young dutch blonde, definately E.European though. [Meadow man, #150]

It was simply a totally different girl and instead of the outstanding model-like beauty on Siren's web site, I encountered a shy, reserved Hungarian girl that can best be described as the nice girl next door. Pardon me, but if I make contact over a card in a phone-box, paying 50 Pounds for the service, I simply know that the lady I am going to meet will hardly be the same as the gorgeous model on the card. However, when I do my booking with one of the most expensive agencies in London, paying 300 Pounds for the hour, I should expect to get the real thing. I mean why bother? - Why not advertise with picks of Claudia Schiffer and Cindy Crawford in the first place, if you know you send your client a totally different girl anyway? [Newmessage, #167]

Sometimes the reality of paying for sex simply does not meet men's expectations, for example:

Cindy was described over the phone as an attractive slim brunette 5'8" and 36-24-34. After a couple of minutes, Cindy came into the room. The description was fairly accurate, although her tits were smaller than I was expecting. [Johnny W, #119]

In some instances men describe how women are under-sold, commenting on how photographs often do not 'do justice' to their looks:

I would say Diane looks pretty much as the photos on her web page except that her hair is now a bit longer. [Bowmore, #34]

Although the web site photo album is very good, it just does not do this beauty any justice whatsoever. Around 5ft 9in tall platinum blonde hair with a tremendous figure A STUNNER! ! ! [David Murphy, #55]

As per pictures on web site (well worth a look) – however Jacqui is far prettier when you meet her. [Eddie, #67]

The question of authenticity, however, goes beyond that of misrepresentation towards an account of whether women's bodies, and body parts, are natural or 'fake'. In particular, men are concerned with women's hair and whether or not it has been artificially coloured:

Paula I would think is in her mid thirties and around 5' 4" with dyed blonde hair. [Fireblade, #73]

Peroxide blonde ... [Meadowman, #150]

Long fake blonde hair ... [Chrisso, #45]

... bleached blonde with black roots coming though ... [Cfothar, #42]

These comments are neither positive nor negative, but presented as simple statements of fact. They do, however, highlight the significance of authenticity and, implicitly, convey value judgement. Similar comments are made by men about women's breasts and whether they are 'natural' or not:

What a body!!! Mind blowing ... Got a feeling her boobs came from a clinic though nevertheless what a pair. [Bigshagger, #26]

She'd had a boob job, just one size up from B to C back in April but unlike some, it wasn't obvious to the look or feel – very natural. (Gadgeteer, #79)

nice body but false tits – still a very nice body. [Ray James, #196]

Once again, comments are not necessarily negative but a preference for authenticity is implied. It is worth stepping back and thinking about why, within this context, authenticity is important. Extensive discussion of breasts appears elsewhere (for example, Millstead and Frith, 2003) but it is worth considering here how breasts are invested with social, cultural and political meanings, identified as a marker of womanhood and synonymous with femininity. Perhaps breasts that are not real are less 'womanly' and 'feminine' in comparison to those that are, and thus, perhaps, women with artificial breasts are perceived as lesser women. We can also see from men's accounts that they expect artificial breasts to look and feel different, thus potentially reducing men's own pleasure. A desire for the authentic, rather than the artificial, may also help to make sex workers appear more 'normal', less deviant and may serve to normalize paying for sex.

Fit Bodies

Chapkis (1985) suggests that western cultures idealise a very limited range of female body shapes. Sassatelli (2003) suggests that the ideal female shape is first and foremost defined as 'firm'. Writing about discourses of fitness, Grimshaw argues that:

It fetishes the youthful body ... It fetishizes the thin or hard body, seeing any female softness or fleshiness as disgusting 'flab' ... The ideal body shape is lean and hard, with visible muscle definition. Lean and muscled hips, thighs and arms should ideally be complemented by rounded breasts, not visibly damaged by the ravages of time or childrearing (Grimshaw, 1999, p.96).

On *PunterNet* frequent comments are made as to whether women are toned or firm:

Stunning figure and long blonde hair, age about 30. Slim firm body which she keeps well toned. [#8]

Dressed sexy with heels. Nice smooth skin, amazing legs. Slim but not toned. [#35]

Whilst thin and hard bodies are the ideal, men's accounts also evidence an interest with the 'normal' or 'average'. As others have, of course, argued, our understanding of what is normal or average, desirable or healthy is anything but value-free. For example, Urla and Swedlund (1998), writing about the history of anthropometry, argue that ideal types and standards are both biased and oppressive. The following extracts illustrate men's understanding of what is normal and average:

She is 5'10" mid 20's and well proportioned and attractive. [Foxman, #76]

Size 12-14. Busty. Average height. [Zak00001, #239]

Blonde, good body and figure, size 10/12 Well proportioned. [Da69er, #51]

A fit body is also a seductive body, but – to look seductive – contemporary female bodies should also be tanned. Vannini and McCright suggest that tanning 'connotes positive characteristics such as youthfulness, sexiness, sociability, affluence, and healthfulness' (2004, p.320). In a similar vein, Black and Sharma (2001) also argue that beauty is associated with positive characteristics and that women, in particular, are most likely to be judged by their physical appearance. Indeed, many punters made reference to tanned women within their accounts, specifically mentioning tanned bodies within the more positive reviews. For example:

Tall, tanned absolutely gorgeous! ! [Jeffix, #119]

She is very tanned, nearly all over! And looked good in the lingerie she was wearing. [Lloyd, #137]

If a tanned body communicates the characteristics outlined above what, then, is communicated by a body that is not tanned? Negative reviews of sex workers often mentioned pale bodies, for example:

Rather bland, slim and unattractive, pale skinned. [Alex, #7]

Agreeing with others, our analysis of men's accounts show how they perpetuate and reinforce images of the ideal female body as one which is predominantly fit, toned and tanned.

Maternal Bodies

As Grimshaw (1999) has argued, whilst the thin and toned body is idealised, the body that has been visibly damaged by the ravages of time or childrearing is not. Whilst there are, of course, specialist sex workers who offer 'milk-maid' services, and areas of the sex industry specialising in pregnancy for example, our data indicate that maternal bodies are generally seen as undesirable. In contrast to the descriptions of women who are fit, toned and tanned, men's descriptions of maternal bodies describe the 'sag' and the 'bag':

> Early 30's – short hair. small tits but nice nipples which were very responsive. Pussy au natural. A bit of a saggy tummy. [Womble, #244]

Men's accounts make specific reference to 'wrinkles' and describe women as 'worn':

> Described as 28 year old brunette 36c 26 36. I think the 28 is very optimistic. She has full fairly soft breasts, a reasonably tight cunt, good smooth skin. A few wrinkles and her stomach is a bit saggy. [Desperate Dan, #58]

> plumpish, looks late forties, claims 39, wrinkled stomach which she keeps covered ... I was disappointed to find that Sandy is a lot more "worn" than I had expected. She is either late forties or has had a hard life. She is not thin and dresses to disguise her unattractive stomach. [Rammie, #194]

They also make reference to stretch marks:

> ... she had some of the worst stretch marks on her stomach, that I've ever seen. i know this doesn't bother some guys, but i cant stand them. she is quite self conscious about them too. [Badboy, #15]

> a stretchmark covered fatty stomach which even hung over her leather trousers. [Crikey, #49]

Infrequently, men explicitly refer to women that do not show signs of childbearing, with the implication that this is something good, for example:

> Very good looking blond about 5' 4" good sized boobs. looked great in long gown, basque and stockings. no signs of child bearing age about 29. [Zx-9, #251]

However, our data show that not all men expect sex workers to be thin and toned. Some punters offer a more flattering perspective of women that are not thin, 'young' and toned, although these men were most definitely in the minority:

> mature beautiful plump lady, about 45, a great tan bit of a saggy stomach but i loved it, wat can i say shes a stunner. [Dre, #64]

In the context of pregnancy and the transition to motherhood, Charles and Kerr (1986) have argued that women's bodies change from being perceived as 'ornamental' to being seen as purely 'functional'. Very similarly, Price (1988) suggests that during pregnancy and the transition to motherhood, women shift from being seen as 'seducers' to 'producers'. These analyses illustrate how, in contemporary western cultures, non-maternal bodies are sexualized bodies, whereas the bodies of mothers are not. The classical dichotomy of mother/whore, reflected in the 'producer/seducer' 'functional/ornamental' discourses outlined above, appears to be reflected here also. The bodies of sex workers that show visible signs of maternity directly challenge the dichotomy between mother/whore and between 'good' and 'bad' women. Sex workers are characterized by their availability, their ornamental bodies and their role as seducers of men. However, as we shall discuss in later chapters, it is not solely the maternal body *per se* which is undesirable, but maternity and maternal identity itself.

Exotic Bodies

Migration continues to fill a gap in the labour market commonly known as the 3-Ds; that is, jobs that are dirty, dangerous and difficult. There is thought to be considerable migration into the UK by women who, voluntarily or otherwise, find themselves working in the sex industry. Although accurate figures are not available, the number of migrant sex workers in the UK is thought to be in the thousands. There is also considerable discussion – in the media, and amongst politicians, policy-makers and academics – on the issue of trafficking. However as Taylor, writing in *The Guardian* newspaper argues, sex workers have become a soft target in the panic over asylum and immigration in the UK, and elsewhere: 'Selling sex plus foreign accent does not automatically equal sex slave... both trafficked and non-trafficked women in the sex industry are finding themselves targeted by the immigration and asylum system' (Taylor, 2006). In a Home Office study of outdoor sex work (Hester and Westmarland, 2004) researchers found that the ethnicity of women working in the sex industry echoed that of local populations; that is, predominantly 'white British'. However, the authors acknowledge that the position is likely to be very different for women working indoors.

On *PunterNet* men's accounts were unlikely to refer to either ethnicity or nationality if the sex worker in question appeared to be obviously 'white' or 'British'. However, many men simply described non-white women as 'coloured', for example:

... coloured lady in mid 30's. [Qbf, #192]

Late 20's, coloured, very good figure – nice tits and a trimmed bush. [Wandering Willy, #253]

Other men were slightly more specific and referred to sex workers as 'Black' or 'Asian':

Great looking Black girl, golden coloured complexion ... [Chimney, #44]

Yasmin is a nice looking, 5'5" slim, young 20's Asian woman with long hair, nice legs and a great arse. [Dillon, #60]

Other accounts were more specific and referred to the sex worker's known, or assumed, country of origin:

> Tina is a sweet coloured girl from South Africa, quite short, 5 foot 2 inches? Lovely breasts, 34 B or C. Partly shaven. Biggish, attractive bottom. Pretty face and lovely lips. [Nomddepc, #171]

> Lela is half-Brazilian and English sweetheart in her early twenties. [Jugg head, #123]

There is a long history of predilection for 'exotic' women amongst white western men. For example, Walker argues:

> For centuries the black woman has served as the primary pornographic 'outlet' for white men in Europe and America. We need only think of the black women used as breeders, raped for the pleasure and profit of their owners. We need only think of the license of the 'master' of the slave women enjoyed. But, most telling of all, we need only study the old slave societies of the South to note the sadistic treatment – at the hands of white 'gentlemen' – of 'beautiful young quadroons and octoroons' who became increasingly (and were deliberately bred to become) indistinguishable from white women (Walker, 1981, p.42).

This, Hill Collins (1990) argues, led to the representation of black female sexuality, in particular, as rampant and animal-like. More contemporary accounts of exotic female sexuality also perpetuate structures of imperialism, colonialism and patriarchy. Letherby and Marchbank's (2003) study of internet brides demonstrates how degrees of exoticism are at play and how men are encouraged to select their bride on the basis of her 'otherness'. Any review of pornographic literature either in print or on the net will also reveal a similar picture. Evidence of such predilection is visible on *PunterNet*. For example, in his field report of *Asian Lady* from Nottingham, *Roy Rogers*, describes disappointment when his 'Asian Lady' is, in fact, from the Caribbean:

> Described as half asian, though in fact is not. Petite with brown hair ... Disappointed as over the phone description given was half asian though is actually half carribean. [Roy Rogers, #208]

Lonestar's account of *Shirani* of Croydon shows how men may expect women advertising themselves as 'Asian', 'Indian', and so forth, not to be British:

> Advertised as busty Indian model and although Asian in appearance, she struck me as being a born and raised Brit gal ... [Lonestar, #138]

However, our analyses of the data suggest that the ability to speak English to a reasonable standard was expected. As we explore in later chapters, conversation is an important aspect of establishing intimacy within commercial sex (see Chapter 4). For example:

Eastern European quite dark skinned and dark hair. Basically fat and ugly, but to make matters worse did not speak English. [Big Boy, #21]

Natasha is about 25 years from Russia. 34b-22-32 at 5ft 4inc. She has shoulder length brunette hair and is part shaven below. Language is not a problem as she speaks very good English. [Big K, #22]

Nina was a pretty West Afican (Senegalese) girl who spoke good english. [Peterperfect, #182]

In contrast, whilst many men enjoy, or seek out, women who they would see as 'exotic' the data suggest that others enjoy paying for sex with the 'girl next door', for example:

Jan is in her early 40's very pleasant to look at. Shapely 40d chest (and very real) nice and fit all over tan, gives the impression of any ones next door neighbour. [Yate Gas, #228]

Diane has the most wonderful smile, perfect teeth and very pretty eyes. She is well spoken and looks like the pretty girl next door rather than a catwalk model. [#72]

Sam is a very pretty blonde with an excellent figure and lovely natural breasts. She's been called girl-next-door, but that's a bit unfair, as she could easily model. However, perhaps it comes from her strong Staffordshire accent, which gives little sense of the erotic. [Worshipper, #241]

Type: girl next door, 21 years, slim natural figure, fair complexion. [Newmessage, #167]

The girl next door, whilst not exotic, is also distinct from the pro'. That is, just as many would not regard virtual sex as 'real' sex, sex with the 'girl next door' is more ordinary and potentially less stigmatising than sex with an obvious pro'. In relation to predilection for the exotic, Månsson (1995) suggests that it is easy to see how the stereotypes of Asian women as submissive, African women as savages and Latin-American women as free and easy develop into men's fantasies about otherness; this, Månsson argues, would compensate for the decrease of their masculine sexual power in their daily relationships.

Ageing Bodies

Whilst the sex industry is largely dominated by younger women, women of all ages exchange sex for money. We were interested to explore the way in which men describe women's physical appearance and chronological age. The data suggest that women fall into one of three categories: 'young', 'mature' and 'elderly'.

By far the largest category of women reviewed on *PunterNet* were those who men described as 'young' and the term 'young lady' can be found repeatedly in men's field reports. It is worth noting though that whilst women were variously described as 'lovely girls', 'down-to-earth girls', and 'friendly girls', they were never described as 'young' girls – with all that this implies in relation to underage sex and the explicit remit of *PunterNet* which claims to deal 'only with lawful activities involving consenting adults'. The youngest age referred to in any review is 18 years. For example:

> 18 years of age, blonde hair, blue eyes, gorgeous body. [Shyboy, #222]

> Young (19-21) year old italian girl. Maria has big boobs 34dd and a voluptuous figure. Not fat. boobs very firm. [Mod, #157]

> Young looking 22 yrs 5 6" long dark hair 36 dd slim body very firm well rounded breasts. very good looker. [Ryno, #210]

However, references were sometimes made to women who looked younger than their chronological age, for example:

> She is looking very young (actually she is 21 but looks like 18) and has a slim, natural figure. [Newmessage, #167]

Far fewer men described experiences with either mature, or especially elderly, sex workers. Women who were described as 'mature' were usually in their 30s and 40s. For example:

> Tall fit Blonde, past sell by date, will fade completely in next few years. Good 36. [Reuters, #199]

> As I entered i was greeted by 2 Mature ladies. The first was about 40. Full rounded figure dressed in a white baby doll outfit stockings & suspenders. Gina, 40's good firm body dressed in black, who i chose. [Naian, #164]

It may be that these descriptive terms are indicative of men's desire for younger women, or, it may be that they reflect the demographics of men who contribute to *PunterNet*, indicating that they are more likely to be at the younger end of the range. 'Elderly' women were in their 50s and beyond, for example:

> Elderly (late 50's) but in good shape. [Jack Parker, #106]

One man describes the more elderly sex worker as one for the 'gentleman':

> Slim, attractive, probably early fifties. Katherine is one for the gentlemen. She advertises herself as pretty and, with the lights dimmed, she looked quite fit. [Tricky Dicky, #233]

> Emma is a mature lady, who will please any gentleman. She has a slim figure, small but perfectly formed breasts, and stands at about 5' 7" tall. [Bfj, #20]

As the above extracts show, older women are brought into the cultural norm by the way in which men describe them as old, yet still attractive and possessing all, if not some, of the physical features of younger women. This was true for women defined as elderly as well as those women still in their 30s, for example:

Fiona is aged around 30 but actually looks a little younger, she has a very firm 36C figure. [Tonto, #231]

Linda is around late 30's but has the body of a teenager. [Okydokey, #173]

We suggest that men's accounts of older women serve not necessarily to flatter the women they have visited (although this may be true in some cases) but to demonstrate that they have high standards, thus serving to maintain an appropriate masculine identity. Fairhurst reminds us that society tends to define women in terms of their physical appearance and that, following on from this 'women's physical appearance is the pivot of her identity *qua* female' (1998, p.259). Men's accounts highlight the way in which youth, attractiveness and chronological age are connected. They also highlight the relationship between age, identity and experience. For example, men who preferred mature or elderly women also tended to explain this preference in terms of purported experience or better technique:

Alexandra describes herself as a mature naturist masseuse. She's blonde, mid 40s, full bodied (her words), busty and has a lovely smile. If you're looking for a 19 year old dolly bird, forget it. But if you want someone who knows her stuff, she's the one. [Beardyone, #18]

If you are after an 18 year old with rock hard boobs then don't bother. If you are looking for a REAL woman with maturity, a sense of humour, and a real feeling for what turns a man on, then Chelsea is for you. [Drummer, #65]

Lesley, may not be the youngest/freshest face at the parlour, but her service comes straight out of the top drawer. [Penfold, #180]

Whilst it is widely acknowledged that men can age fairly gracefully, women are confronted by an aesthetics which values youth. Our analyses of the data would suggest that this largely holds true but that there are some exceptions to this.

Women, the Net and Representation

Cyberspace has been heralded as an opportunity for change in the social order of late, or post, modern societies. The increasing presence of sex workers and their clients on the net suggest an opportunity for change in the power relations of paid-for-sex. Arguably, cyberspace offers sex workers a new opportunity for representation. However, it is clear from the frequently pornographic images displayed that, in marketing their sexual services, sex workers and their agents subscribe to the commonly prevailing representations of female sexual availability and draw on conventional racialised notions of female attractiveness.

It should perhaps not surprise us that the characteristics which women seem most keen to accentuate in their internet representations are those which are of most interest to potential clients. Appearance is obviously central, but personality and sexual preferences also play a significant part. At the same time, there is evidence of women using the internet to lay down 'ground-rules' for commercial sexual encounters, which arguably would not have been possible prior to the emergence of the internet – or, at least, not in the same way. Price, terms and conditions for payment, and sexual limits are all commonly advertised on women's websites, which may be interpreted as something of a redress in the balance of power, albeit perhaps a minor one. Within the context of commodification, it is also worth noting how sex workers commodify men. For example, Phoenix (2000) draws on the narratives of female sex workers to show how they view men 'as money'.

We have tried to show in this chapter that the emergence of the net has the potential to transform at least one small part of the sex industry. Sex workers themselves are increasingly making use of the net to market their services, and to assume greater control than has hitherto been possible over the ways in which they represent themselves to potential clients and to the world in general. This development is open to a number of possible interpretations. On the one hand, we might choose to regard it as liberating, and see the greater control exercised by sex workers over how they are represented as something of a redress in the balance of power between sex worker and client (or, perhaps, more globally, between men and women). On the other, we may see this development as a further insidious refinement in an ever-increasing drive to reduce women's bodies to mere commodities and the pursuit of McSex.

Chapter 4

Intimacy, Emotion and Romance

Why Do Men Pay for Sex?

Why do men pay for sex? This question is difficult to answer fully since our knowledge and understanding of the punter is so very limited. Monto (2000) argues that this is also a difficult question because both lay people and those who research men who pay for sex tend to assume that they already know the reasons why men seek out sex workers; he argues that 'people tend to assume that the motives of johns are obvious, not worthy of serious exploration' (2000, p.76). Our knowledge of sex work is also contradictory, for example, whilst Kinsey's (1998) research (originally published in 1948) would support the idea that most men would pay for sex if they could, more recent research suggests that paying for sex is neither a conventional nor a terribly widespread activity (Johnson and Mercer, 2001). So, what do we know about the reasons men pay for sex?

There is now a growing body of literature on what Campbell (1998) calls the 'invisible men', or what Sullivan and Simon (1998) have described as the 'unseen patrons of prostitution'. Many of these studies are motivated by a desire to explore men's motivations in paying for sex. McKeganey and Barnard (1996), for example, studied the motivations of 70 men in Glasgow, United Kingdom and found that they reported a desire for specific sexual acts, as well as enjoying the clandestine and illicit nature of commercial encounters. Other researchers (for example, Monto, 1991) have also identified a desire for specific sexual acts, particularly fellatio, and cite this as one of the fundamental reasons for visiting a sex worker. These studies support the idea that men pay for specific sexual acts that they are less likely to 'get at home'. However, a telephone survey carried out in Melbourne, Australia (Louie et al., 1998) found that 32 per cent of callers cited good sex as the major motivation of men who pay for sex, followed by convenience, which was mentioned by 20 per cent of callers. In another survey of 612 men in Victoria, Australia (Pitts et al., 2004) nearly 44 per cent of men felt that commercial sex offered them 'relief' – in some ways this reflects traditional, and popular, discourses of a male sex 'drive' and the idea that sex workers are performing a service within society. In the same survey, another 20 per cent of men stated that they were often under the influence of alcohol or drugs when they paid for sex.

Explanations are most likely numerous as well as subtle since there is no one clear motive that applies universally. Like others before her, Campbell (1998) has also found that the majority of men have more than one motivation for paying for sex. However, just as others have identified, commercial sex is not simply the exchange of sex for money (McKeganey and Barnard, 1996; Chapkis, 1997). That is, commercial sex also involves emotional exchange, and the development of relationships based on notions of love, intimacy and romance. Whilst 'sex', 'love' and 'intimacy' are analytically separate, they are, within people's social practices, inextricably linked.

The concept of 'intimacy' – or 'intimacy theory' – has considerable contemporary currency (Giddens, 1992). It refers to a specific kind of knowing, loving and closeness to another person, of talking, listening and sharing. This type of intimacy refers to an intimacy of the self, rather than of the body, though bodily intimacy may be seen to enhance emotional intimacy. Although the term 'intimacy' can be a euphemism for sexual intercourse (Jordan, 2004), Jamieson (1998) suggests that intimacy is composed of several dimensions. Firstly, intimacy can refer to the close association of individuals leading to the acquisition of familiarity. Secondly, it refers to the possession of detailed knowledge of each other which nobody else has. Intimacy also refers to notions of knowing and understanding and to the development of trust between individuals. Finally, Jamieson suggests that loving, caring and sharing are also dimensions of intimacy.

Within certain forms of sexual behaviour, intimacy is thought to be lacking. For example, Jamieson (1998) argues that within paid-for sex, 'sex' and 'intimacy' are totally separate. However, we would question this. Whilst intimacy does not play a central part in every commercial encounter, it is a key component of many. And whilst not all dimensions of intimacy may be equally apparent, the notion of intimacy does serve to structure men's accounts of their commercial sexual experiences.

This chapter explores men's accounts of intimacy, emotion and romance within the context of paying for sex. It also explores the role played by intimacy, emotional labour and emotion work in the management of a potentially deviant identity.

The Commodification of Intimacy: Performing Erotic Labour

It is now well established that the performance of erotic labour involves the commodification of intimacy and emotion. In Chapter 1 we explored how the emotional labour of sex is an important part of the debate surrounding sex work. Drawing on her work on flight attendants, Hochschild (1983) offers two concepts in relation to how emotions are managed: emotion work and emotional labour. The concept of emotion work presupposes that individuals are capable of, if not habitually engaging in, the reflection and shaping of their innermost feelings. Hochschild describes emotion work as the 'act of trying to change in degree or quality an emotion or feeling ... Note that "emotion work" refers to the effort – the act of trying – and not to the outcome, which may or may not be successful' (1979, p.561). She describes emotional labour as 'the management of feeling to create a publicly observable facial and bodily display; emotional labour is sold for a wage and therefore has exchange value' (Hochschild, 1983, p.7).

Writing about emotion in sex work O'Neill argues:

Emotional labour is a central aspect of the working women's relationship with their clients. Emotional energy is directed at minimizing their own feeling worlds at work, and emotional energy is used in and around their interactions with and for clients ... women have to be good at 'gentling' men, at flattering, counselling and consoling the male ego while at the same time providing his ideal fantasy woman, even though he may make her 'feel sick' (O'Neill, 2001, pp.142-3).

Some researchers have argued that whilst sex workers are selling sexual services, intimacy is not one of these services. Others note that intimacy is more likely to be offered by women working as escorts, or in other forms of indoor sex work, compared to women who work on the streets (Lever and Dolnick, 2000). As we have seen in Chapter 3, emotional labour has clear exchange value within the sex industry and is openly marketed within the indoor sex trade.

Drawing on Maurer's (1940) *The Big Con*, Goffman's (1952) work on the confidence game – or the con – is useful here in that he argues that the con is 'practiced on private persons by talented actors who methodically and regularly build up informal social relationships just for the purpose of abusing them' (p.451). An important part of the con, after the victim has been reeled in and then exploited, is 'cooling the mark out'; the term 'mark' referring to the victim of such a con. Cooling the mark involves handling an individual whose conception of him/herself has been compromised. So, is sex work a con?

There have been numerous studies exploring the con in relation to the sex industry. Pasko (2002), for example, focuses on stripping as a confidence game, suggesting that, within this context, intimacy is counterfeit, or false. In relation to strippers, she argues: 'From the flirtatious pull of her garter to the counterfeiting of emotional intimacy, the stripper, or exotic dancer, entices and entertains customers through a complex negotiation of power' (pp.49-50). Pasko argues that as a sexual ideal, strippers wield considerable power during social interactions with punters. However, as Goffman (1952) notes, individuals often do not think of themselves as someone who can be taken in by anything or anyone. As in any con game, a stripper will need to cool her mark out, leaving him with the belief that she was genuinely interested in him.

Goffman's (1959) notion of the 'cynical performance' is also useful here as a description of 'a social actor with little belief in the performance but who uses the performance and the elicited convictions of the audience to achieve other ends' (p.17). Drawing on this, Sijuwade's (1995) study of topless dancing provides a useful illustration of the way in which the cynical performance is constructed through the creation of counterfeit intimacy. Counterfeit intimacy, Sijuwade argues, is established firstly by the 'setting'; the physical layout and its background items which provide the appropriate props to establish a feeling of intimacy. As we discuss below, in *PunterNet* men spend considerable time describing intimate settings and the romantic props – candlelight, music, champagne – which form the background items. 'Appearance' is also important and within the context of a topless club: 'The waitress-dancer must give the appearance to patrons that this is indeed a recreational activity from them while simultaneously conducting what is most assuredly work for her' (p.372). Her manner is also important in that she must give the impression of enjoyment and availability.

Thus, the literature is widely supportive of the idea that sex workers engage in emotional labour. Indeed, Sanders' (2004a) study of sex workers in Birmingham, UK, highlighted that the management of emotion posed a more significant and more persistent problem than the management of any other risks, including the management of risks to health and physical safety. In many instances this emotional labour appears to be successful, for example:

> Angie is very chatty and will trust you with info most working girls would not which makes you feel special, family life etc. [Legman, #134]

> Afterwards we chatted for a while – nothing contrived. [Daveinascot, #54]

As Wood's (2000) research in strip clubs shows, 'making men feel special' is one of the ways in which sex workers try to make punters feel important or desired and, thus, in the case of stripping, good tippers. The data above appear to indicate that men believe sex workers to be genuine in this expression of intimacy and emotion. In other cases, men become well aware of the cynical performance, as our data show:

> ... she welcomed me and was friendly in a chat-line, scripted, type of way. Whilst I was comfortable enough, I always felt that everything she was telling me about her lifestyle was false or exaggerated with the aim of turning me on. [Rammie, #194]

> As my hands wandered over body afterwards, I told her (truthfully) that would never forget what had happened between us. 'I won't either', she said – the only wrong move she made. [Morgan, #158]

In these instances whilst women are clearly engaging in emotional labour they are not doing so successfully.

We can, however, ask ourselves whether it is only sex workers who manage their emotions. Writing specifically about escort work, Lever and Dolnick (2000, p.86) suggest that: 'The client understands that being intimate is part of the call girl's work and that he is not her only client. Both client and call girl agree to pretend that her caring and sexual attraction for him are real.' Implicit in this is the suggestion that men are complicit in their manipulation and that they, too, engage in emotion work. However our data show no evidence of such complicity in that men either seem to believe in the display of intimacy, or, became aware of their part in the con game.

Sex, Romance and Intimacy

Intimacy, Knowing and Relationships

We now turn to men's accounts of romance and intimacy. Previous studies have shown that some men find that paying for sex provides them with the opportunity of having sex with a large number of different women. For example, McKeganey and Barnard (1996, p.51), writing about the punters in their Glasgow study state: 'Some men drew attention to the fact that before they were married they had been sexually involved with large numbers of women and they wished to continue this without the complications of maintaining a fully fledged affair or series of affairs'. As we have discussed in Chapter 3, Campbell's (1998) study of men in Liverpool, UK also shows that paying for sex allows men to choose women with particular physical characteristics.

Our data indicate that some men form long-term commercial relationships with sex workers, not because of a fear of HIV – or for any other reason – but due to a sense of loyalty and a sense of comforting familiarity. For example, one individual describes a twelve year relationship with sex worker, *Alexandra*:

> I've been seeing Alexandra for about twelve years (we worked it out the other day) and I have a wonderful time every time I see her. She meets me at the door, usually dressed in a housecoat and nothing else, undone down the front. We have a kiss, then a chat, then into her bedroom with its big double bed. She gives an excellent massage, lovely oral and sex in every position you want. An absolute delight ... [Beardyone, #18]

Other relationships range from months to years, for example:

> I've been to see Lindsey many times over the years and so this report is an amalgam of all my visits. [Tommo, #230]

> I've been seeing this lady for about 2 years and keep going back. [Lw, #141]

> I have visited Tina a number of times and find her very exciting. [Nomdepc, #171]

Even when men do not form long-term relationships in real time, importance is placed on a sense of 'knowing' and familiarity and, as Jamieson (1998) notes, these are feelings implicit to the development of intimacy between individuals. *Eddie* describes this:

> Jacqui is very friendly and makes you feel very relaxed. We chatted for ages and it felt like I had known her for years. [Eddie, #67]

Of course, the development of such intimacy is not central to all men, neither has it been reported by all other researchers (for example, Campbell, 1998). The aptly named punter, *Onetrack* states:

Yana's english is not perfect but we were able to share a joke and even have a short conversation on Russian authors (I wanted to get laid not talk). [Onetrack, #174]

As prior research has indicated, some men specifically engage in commercial sex with the purpose of avoiding intimacy (McKeganey and Barnard, 1996, Campbell, 1998). Within this context, paying for sex is perceived as a convenient way of avoiding the trappings of intimate relationships.

Other scholars have highlighted instances of sex workers and punters establishing relationships after meeting within a commercial setting. As one respondent in Warr and Pyett's (1999) Australian study states: 'I was working one night ... and he happened to drive past. He was on his way home ... and he said he noticed me and came around, back around and went around the block, and there was [sic] about eight cars ... and something just made me take notice of him and his eyes. I just fell in love ...' (pp.298-9). Of course, this kind of experience is unlikely to be common and we found no instances of this in our own research. However in a study of call girls in Los Angeles, USA Monto (2000) notes that – as in other commercial relationships – the longer individuals know each other the greater the likelihood of a genuine intimate exchange. He states 'not all the call girls are being "phony" or acting all of the time' (p.98). So, within this context, genuine intimacy can be seen as a kind of customer loyalty.

Ritualized Courtship and Romantic Settings

Plummer (1975) argues that there exists a range of sexual meanings which include the utilitarian, the erotic, the romantic and the symbolic. He suggests that these categories often overlap with one another serving both in the construction of sexual meanings and the organisation of sexual life. Sexuality, he argues, can be manifested in a symbolic form to provoke feelings of sexiness, highlight gender differences or demonstrate notions of love. The romantic symbols of modern ritualized courtship are infused with all of these. Writing about non-commercial masculinity and heterosexual scripts, Wyatt Seal and Ehrhardt argue that courtship 'may be defined as the process or set of behaviours that precedes and elicits sexual behaviour' (2003, p.295). The typical symbols, or props, of non-commercial heterosex might include soft candlelight, soft music, food, wine, and so on; all of these serving to create an ambience of romantic courtship. Some of the accounts on *PunterNet* would be difficult to distinguish from such imagery, for example:

We met, we ate a lovely lasagne (Charise loves Italian food!), we drank wine. We talked. We played some music. We took our time. [Entranced, #69]

The qualities of intimacy are captured by this concept of romance (Warr, 2001). Whilst intimacy is often thought to be a largely female preoccupation, others have suggested that this is an outdated perspective. For example, in a paper titled *Girls Want Sex, Boys Want Love*, which focuses on the discourses of sexuality of young people, Allen (2003) suggests that whilst young men are more likely to be interested in intercourse than young women, they are also interested in relationships that are caring, supportive and understanding. Just as romantic love and intimacy have been shown to play a crucial role in extending women's pleasure in non-commercial sex (for example, see Jackson, 1993 and Holland *et al.,* 1991), romance and intimacy play an important part of men's pleasure in paying for sex. According to Wyatt Seal and Ehrhardt (2003), the 'courtship game' commonly includes small talk. Men's cyber-stories show how commercial sex often follows a courtship script similar to that of non-commercial heterosex:

> Anyway, we had some wine and a lengthy chat and then strawberries and cream ...
> [Rumblingtum, #209]

Men also commonly report being offered a drink of some sort on arrival, sometimes wine or beer, or a cold drink, and sometimes tea or coffee. Within commercial encounters, having a drink serves a number of purposes. For example:

> The receptionist made me feel very relaxed – drink – porno and mags available ... [Rega3, #198]

It is also an expected preamble and part of a ritualized system of courtship. As with any exchange, commercial or otherwise, a drink can be used as a form of relaxation, serving to put an individual at their ease and is an activity typical of real dates (Lever and Dolnick, 2000), as *Okydoky* describes:

> We chatted over a few drinks for a while then we went up to her bedroom ... [Okydoky, #173]

In parlours and walk-ups, or any environment managed by a receptionist or maid, drinks are sometimes offered whilst men wait for the previous punter to leave. For example *Macman* states:

> i was offered a drink by the maid although I did not have to wait long. [Macman, #142]

Within commercial sex a drink also bridges the transition between commercial negotiation and sexual experience, as Jay states:

> After talking for a little bit, and a quick drink and handing over money we got down to business. [Jay, #109]

> She spent about 15 minutes sorting out the money, getting towels and a glass of champagne for me, while chatting and making me feel much more relaxed. [Anon Chris, #10]

In Sanders' (2004a) study, 45 of the 55 women she interviewed always took payment before the business, hiding or stashing it with someone else. Whilst being offered a drink is perceived by men as a 'nice touch', it is also a technique which keeps men busy whilst women put their money safely away. *Coach* states:

She took the money and offered me a drink as she left the room, nice touch. [Coach, #47]

Men's accounts also make reference to other romantic props, such as the use of candles or soft music, as Adrian and Alan both note:

Very friendly and made every attempt to make you feel relaxed from the start. Comfortable bedroom, clean, candles, and soft music. [Adrian, #5]

There was candlelight and soft music was playing. [Alan, #6]

Previous research has shown that indoor sex workers frequently report receiving gifts (Lever and Dolnick, 2000) and that this is one of the distinctions between indoor and outdoor sex work. These gifts often include perfume, flowers or champagne which, as Lever and Dolnick note are 'the type of gifts a man might give to a girlfriend or wife' (2000, p.94). However, whilst courtship rituals and romantic symbols play an important role in establishing men's comfort, men's accounts demonstrate that such props also play an important role in extending value, or getting more from the exchange. For example:

... if you really want to get the best from Peaches a few suggestions. Firstly take some champagne with you when you visit – she drinks little else and it makes her very randy. [Valentine, #240]

This is not dissimilar to non-commercial sex in which the 'bottom line dynamic' is often negotiation and exchange for sex. As one of the punters in Campbell's study says: 'Why go through all the hassle of buying drinks for a women, taking her out for a meal when you don't even know if you'll get anywhere? You might as well just pay a prostitute' (1998, p.168).

Romance can be defined as something 'fanciful and unrealistic' and it can be used to 'evoke the wonder and intensity of mutual longing in sexual attraction' (Warr, 2001, p.242). The use of romance as a means of establishing intimacy serves to create an atmosphere of mutual longing, rather than one of worker and punter. Thus, it serves to detract from the fact that this is merely a commercial encounter in which he, the punter, is paying for sex. Sex work, Wilton (199) argues takes its socio-cultural meaning from its position in relation to the 'emotion/commerce boundary'. Since sex should be tied to emotion: 'You are not supposed to pay for sex, nor to charge for it' (p.187). And, as Wilton implies, it is the *commercial* nature and not the *sexual* nature of sex work which is identified as wrong, and which is potentially discrediting to men.

Girlfriend Sex

'Making Love'

Whilst intimacy of one kind or another plays an important part in commercial sex, some experiences stand out from the rest. The following two accounts describe experiences where men make the distinction between feeling like a lover rather than a punter:

> We then got cleaned up and dressed, she was very friendly throughout and really made it feel as if we were new found lovers as opposed to an Escort experience. Will I be back, I have already booked her for an overnight. [Slappy, #226]

> ... the sex was fantastic, she makes you feel like a lover not a punter. [Legman, #134]

This kind of experience is often described by men as 'girlfriend sex', or a 'girlfriend experience'. As Jamieson (1998) notes, notions of love, sharing and caring are characteristic of an intimate relationship. Sex work is often modelled on practices which are central to the concept and norms of heterosexual intimacy (Warr and Pyett, 1999). But, what is a girlfriend experience? Firstly, let us start with an account of what it is not:

> This is not gentle, this is not girlfriend sex, it is frenzied raw physical pleasure. If sex was on at the Olympics, this girl would take home gold ... [Dv, #66]

For some, girlfriend sex is gentle and loving. It is 'making love' rather than 'having sex'. As O'Connell Davidson (1995; 1996) points out, sex workers and their punters alike, exist within a normative moral order where certain meanings are ascribed to human sexuality. These meanings dictate that legitimate sex is that which occurs between men and women who love each other. Indeed Wyatt Seal and Ehrhardt (2003) highlight how men, in their narratives of emotional intimacy often contrast 'having sex' with 'making love'. For example, one of their respondents stated: 'Making love is different than just up and down sex. You put yourself into it, caressing her while you're doing this and make her feel good and she's making you feel good, and there's a lot of life and love there, not just sex' (Wyatt Seal and Ehrhardt, 2003, p.307). As punters *Winkle* and *Entranced!* state:

> Wow it was like making love to a girlfriend of a kind she was so passionate and involved. [Winkle, #247]

> I suppose the best I can say is that it was more like making love than having sex ... the nicest – in every sense – girl I've met for absolutely ages. [Entranced! #69]

Other men seem to concur with this kind of distinction too. In stark contrast to previous research findings, they refer to cuddling and describe feelings of being loved and cared for:

I was after a 'girlfriend' experience and Barbie plays this part to perfection, giving lots and lots of love, and attention, and forever asking if you are ok (YES!!) This young lady has it all, looks, personality, brains and a terrific sense of humour an absolute joy to be with. [David Murphy, #55]

There are lots of cuddles and she actually appears to enjoy the sex ... The well used term 'girlfriend sex' seems to be totally appropriate here. Without being crude, Tiff feels superb whilst 'inside'. I'11 be back as soon as possible. I came away feeling great and had to phone her back and tell her. [Visitor, #237]

Brewis and Linstead (2000) highlight the distinction between three types of sexual encounter: relational sex, work sex and recreational sex. They argue that relational sex refers to the type of sex reserved for partners and 'being in love'. Work sex, or sex work, is purely physical and uninvolved, whereas recreational sex is that reserved for private and impersonal sex, as in the case of a one-night stand. In the UK television programme, *Vice: The Sex Trade* (ITV, 1998) masseuse *Karen* describes the distinction between relational sex and sex work. She says 'With a client it's not really feelings. You can still enjoy it but there's not actually any emotion ... at the end of the day you're just having sex and that's it. There's no feelings. Once it's over, it's over, whereas with your boyfriend you'd still be snuggled up ... whereas you wouldn't do that with a client'. In their study of sex work in New Zealand, Weatherall and Priestley (2001) also note that men who pay for sex distinguish between 'real'/ relational sex and 'pretend'/work sex. For example, one punter is reported as only having penis-vagina intercourse standing up because he believed that 'real' sex was done lying down – and by having only pretend sex he still remained faithful to his wife. Thus, a girlfriend experience can be seen to simulate relational, rather than work, sex.

Kissing

Kissing is also often referred to within the context of Girlfriend Sex and men are prepared to pay more for it, as *Delboy* explains:

£60 is £15 over the odds ... but it included the extras of kissing (very good, not just once or twice but all through the session). [Delboy, #57]

However, previous research indicates that sex workers are aware that by commanding higher prices this often means that kissing is the price they pay. For example, one of the calls girls quoted in the study by Lever and Dolnick (2000, p.96) highlights the distinction between indoor and outdoor sex work stating: 'The street women are just selling sex, they don't have to play the games that we do. We make believe we want to be with the guy, and if you want to be with him, then you'd want to kiss him right? Guys expect a lot for a lot of money'. As discussed in Chapter 3, when searching for sex on the net, it is usually possible to search specifically for women who do kissing

Kissing can also form part of the contractual negotiations and by offering to kiss, sex workers can attract clients, as exemplified by *Reuters'* complaint:

> Lied on phone by promising kissing. [Reuters, #199]

For others, kissing is what specifically demarcates ordinary paid-for-sex from girlfriend sex:

> All the way through we had been kissing so this was a real girlfriend experience. I can't wait to see her again what a jewel she is. [SharpShooter, #221]

Kissing is integral to intimacy, and to the whole concept of a girlfriend experience since kissing is strongly related to more relational notions of sex. Indeed, Brewis and Linstead argue that many sex workers will not kiss because, 'it is too similar to the kind of behaviour in which she would engage with a non-commercial sexual partner, it smacks too much of genuine desire and love for the other person' (2000, p.215). They argue that, by not kissing, sex workers are able to erect both physical and emotional barriers which serve to safeguard identity. Men sometimes believe that sex workers will kiss selectively – that is, they will kiss some punters but not others. For example:

> Into the bedroom – she is a selective kisser – it seems if she genuinely likes you then kissing is on the menu and very passionate it is too, otherwise not. [#246]

If men are able to secure, or pay for, kissing then it may make them feel special. This may tell them something about themselves and serve to positively reinforce their self-identity. However, as previous research has identified, 'regulars' are often afforded special privileges not offered to other punters. For example, a study of call girls in Los Angeles, USA (Lever and Dolnick, 2000) suggested that 'regulars' were more likely to get 'sleepovers' and were often not charged for time not spent engaged in non-sexual activities, such as having dinner. In spite of the relative importance of kissing, it has received very little sociological attention. Tiefer (1995) comments on this by explaining how when she carried out a literature search on kissing she found a couple of papers referring to mononucleosis, an article on the fish known as the 'kissing gourami' and unrelated work written by people with names such as Kissler. She states that, 'Even sex researchers are uninterested. *Sex* now refers to intercourse, not kissing or petting' (p.77). We, too, found a similar dearth of literature on the subject of the kiss.

Passion, Love and Spontaneity

Although some men believe girlfriend sex to be a more loving experience, girlfriend sex is also less formulaic and more spontaneous. *Fboc* [#72] said: 'I told her to throwaway the rulebook'. It is passionate rather than contrived:

On turning me over, Katie changed into something of a nymphomaniac. Katie had no reservations about chewing nipples, kissing with tongues, cuddling, rolling around, giving a BBBJ (not to completion) and talking about dirty fantasies. I have to say that she does a wonderful job of transforming paid sex into something far more exciting and memorable. [Seanjohnstone, #217]

Tia is a very sexy lady and she will do almost anything within reason including 'a' and 'owo' and swallow too! I took everything, and without any sense of crudeness. If you like a great figure on long, shapely legs and a fantastic, girlfriend type occasion, Tia is the one to choose. [Jim Henson, #133]

For some, girlfriend sex is the ultimate experience – the 'Holy Grail' of the sex industry – something sought after but diffuse and unclear. *Casca*, describing one of the few accounts of couple escorting, is uncertain about whether his experience was a true 'girlfriend experience':

Lisa & Steve are a very attractive couple in their mid 20's who are swingers and have just started escorting, which is great for the rest of us. This was my first foray into a threesome and both of them made it comfortable, horny and most of all 'fun' ... The only question I have in my mind is can it be a true Girlfriend experience if her husband is actively participating? This was as close as it gets, I'd say. [Casca, #41]

It is only really in the last 20 years or so that sociologists have paid attention to the concept of 'love'. Love is part of public culture, and it is socially and culturally constructed rather than solely personal and private. Jackson (1993) makes the distinction between 'falling in love' and 'being in love', and drawing on Hite's (1988) study notes that whilst people in long term relationships may not be 'in love' with their partners, they do say that they 'love' them. In his work on intimacy, Giddens (1992) also draws a distinction between passionate love and romantic love; the former evoking fervour and danger and the latter being something that is normatively desirable. In men's sexual stories of commercial sex we see descriptions of both.

However, as argued elsewhere, sexual stories are gendered. Jackson, for example, argues that ' ... men are not encouraged to develop competence in locating themselves within discourses of the emotions ... It is through the idiom of sexual bravado and conquest, not the language of romance, that masculinity is asserted' (1993, p.214). In Redman's (2001) study of love, romance and schooling, however, boys' investment in romantic love can be understood as a way of engaging in an adult form of heterosexual masculinity. Within paid-for sex, perhaps love assumes a different role. We can see that men adopt the language of romance in their stories of paying for sex and we contend that this is one of the ways in which some of the men who pay for sex assert their masculinity and attempt to locate themselves outside of deviant identity.

Decency, Privacy and Respect

Just as it is often considered rude to discuss one's private sexual experiences, especially those occurring within marriage or a committed relationship, the girlfriend experience is similarly constrained. In many of the accounts in which men describe girlfriend sex there is a reluctance to disclose personal and intimate details. Sometimes this appears to be at the request of the sex worker, or at least it is presented as being in her best interests:

> This versatile and accommodating lady will not be rushed, she will do almost anything to please her visitor, and on this occasion her visitor's pleasure seemed genuinely to please her too. Took her time building up to the main course which was truly memorable. No details of our intimate moments, in respect of the lady's request. [Altosax, #8]

> I don't think she would appreciate me giving too much details ... but suffice to say, I had a great time, especially her oral skills were particularly good. Treat her well ... she is a real gem. [Platinum, #186]

In other accounts it is presented more as a form of common decency:

> I'm not going into graphic detail about our time together but will say this, I am not the youngest rooster about yet Andrea made me feel very special indeed. From the company and conversation to the very most exquisite and frankly explosive physical moments we shared I always felt she truly cared for and was interested in me. It would be all to easy to see Andrea every day, if my wallet and heart would take it rd do it, what more can I say. She is one in a million, treat her well and you will be rewarded in kind. [Richard French, #200]

> ... I have to keep reminding myself that I am not reporting my own girlfriend's personal and intimate details to the world, and that Zena's a business women, and I am writing a recommendation. [Richy, #201]

> Not wishing to disclose too many personal details – but suffice to say Paula's speciality is her 'A' level, where I believe she passed with honours, and as I've already said I'm a 'bum' man, and so this was a great experience. [Fireblade, #73]

> I am not going to go into a vast detail of what we did, none of your business, but she was great. [#165]

Ultimately, girlfriend sex is all about an experience which does not feel like the man is having to pay for it. It is a commercial exchange designed and enacted to be experienced as a non-commercial encounter:

> This was my first experience of a visiting escort, well any escort and I was blown away by the quality of her, I did not feel like any money had been exchanged ... [Expresstrain, #71]

Amazing lady stunning body and really knows how to use it. What a pussy and a brilliant blowjob nice to see a girl not pull away when you cum. More like girlfriend sex than paid sex. Will see her again soon. [Kovac, #131]

There is also often a reluctance to 'share' a sex worker with others. There is evidence of jealousy and a desire for – though not the elusion of – exclusivity:

The only sadness is that after this review I may have to share her with more of you. [Nealmort, #165]

Great girlfriend like sex. We finished up in a heap of very sweaty tangled bodies. She is one sexy lass. Hands off. [#72]

For many sex workers, these types of punter fall into the category of the 'romantics': men who fall in love with a sex worker or who confuse work sex with genuine love and intimacy. In McKeganey and Barnard one sex worker says about these types: 'Oh I hate that, really that is ma hate, when they try and get all lovey dovey. I mean t'me any guy that tries to get lovey dovey with a prostitute is off his head ... You always get the one that's "I really like you and why are you doing this ..." and I just hate that.' (1996, p.89).

Intimacy and the Management of Emotional Risk

Plummer (1975) argues that individuals who may be potentially identified as deviant have three broad choices in their management of this: denial (refusing to see themselves or be identified as deviant); diffusion (becoming aware of their deviance but finding it reprehensible); and, deference (coming to accept the deviancy) but it is denial and deference which are most relevant here.

Accounts which rationalize behaviour as 'normal' and serve to neutralize deviancy can be interpreted as a form of denial. This denial serves to prevent 'good' men from seeing themselves as 'bad' as a consequence of their deviant actions. Thus, men who pay for sex can come to see themselves as engaging in a deviant act whilst not necessarily considering themselves to be fundamentally deviant. Counter reactions in the form of 'moral crusades' (Plummer, 1975) are also a form of denial in that they place deviant individuals in direct juxtaposition to the values normally associated with a deviant act. In the case of sex work, paying for sex is associated with sleazy desperation, as well as violence and abuse. Popular images of sex workers concentrate on outdoor sex work and street sex workers, who are typically held to be 'amoral, conspicuously vulgar and indiscriminate and a lost and hopeless victim of abusers and manipulators' (Scambler, 1997, p.105). These images can be found in the academic literature, in government documents and reports, and in the media. Just as men's reluctance to disclose personal and intimate details can be seen as a form of common decency, so, too, is their tendency to ask other men to treat particular sex workers 'with respect'. For example:

Had a great time and no doubt will be back. Be nice to her chaps – she deserves it! [Big Bad Boy, #23]

... we finished the bottle of wine and had a short talk. I have t! o say that Lela is a beautiful, intelligent and well-spoken lady worth her weight in gold. If you ever visit her treat her with respect and admiration because she deserves it. [Jugg head, #123]

During the session Racquel was gentle and loving and did not rush things in any way, she is obviously a special lady treat her well. [Alan, #6]

The idea of treating someone with respect was also extended to types of sex act. For some men, asking women to participate in anything other than 'straight' activities – for example, defecation – would be considered disrespectful:

Treat her with respect guys – she will not do dom, 'brown or water' just straight wonderful sex. [Punterex, #191]

All in all this was two hours of intimate bliss. A great girl who worked hard to give me a good time. Treat her with the respect she clearly deserves and enjoy every minute of her company. Finally to all those readers with slightly perverse tastes, don't bother this girl – she is pure CLASS and above that sort of thing. [Adrian, #5]

Whilst contributing to *PunterNet* appears to be a public acknowledgement of both deviant behaviour, and a deviant identity, these counter reactions may serve as recognition of the deviant act but not necessarily of a deviant identity. It makes a distinction between the 'good' men who engage in 'bad' behaviour and the 'bad' men.

However, the call to treat someone well is also another means of manipulating the exchange, and of getting women to do more for them. For example:

Paula is a real pleasure to be with and I'm sure if you treat her right, she would be game for almost anything – a real class act! I shall certainly be seeing her again in the not too distant future. [Fireblade, #73]

She is very friendly when treated well. [Jode1, #115]

So far we have established that, at least from men's perspectives, commercial sex not only includes intimacy but that intimacy can be a central feature of men's experiences. Within the sex industry, the concept of risk is normally associated with physical risk, especially the risk of HIV – which we examine in Chapter 7 – but also the risk of violence and abuse. Within discourses of risk, emotional risk is less well researched and when it has been studied, it has focused on the emotional labour performed by sex workers (Sanders, 2004a). However, as we have argued above, commercial sex also involves emotional exchange, and the development of relationships based on the concepts of love, intimacy and romance. Men who pay for sex may not perform emotional labour but they do engage in emotion work. This emotion work serves to structure their experiences of commercial sex and plays a role in the management of identity.

Whilst men do not appear to be complicit with the notion of a cynical performance they, too, engage in the commodification of intimacy for their own ends. There were many examples of this within men's accounts:

Guys, treat her with respect and you will be rewarded. [MikeyP, #155]

... treat her nice and she will return the favour. [Minge Eater, #156]

So treat them right and you will get the right response in return. [Nig2259, #169]

... please treat these ladies with respect and they will please you beyond your dreams, fail and they will shun you. [Mr T., #161]

So, just as sex workers engage in the commodification of intimacy, punters are aware that 'treating her nice' can bring them considerable erotic and intimate gains.

Although men are aware of the advantages of manipulating emotion they often believe in the intimacy displayed by female sex workers. Whilst there may be some commercial relationships in which sex workers feel genuine intimacy, and this seems most likely both within long term relationships and within indoor, rather than outdoor, work, performing erotic labour must be recognized as the quintessential con game.

Chapter 5

Sexual Pleasure and Erotic Performance

'Just A Good Hard Shag'

It is widely acknowledged that commercial sex involves the commodification of emotional intimacy, but physical pleasure and erotic performance are also important elements of the commercial encounter. In contrast to many of the accounts described in Chapter 4, not all men are concerned with exchanging emotional intimacy, nor with having a Girlfriend Experience. Some are more concerned with realizing an erotic sexual experience – or 'a good hard shag':

> This woman is dynamite! I visited her once at Liasons and was as good if not better this time round. This is not gentle, this is not girlfriend sex, it is frenzied raw physical pleasure. If sex was on at the olympics, this girl would take home gold for the emerald isle ... I left knackered, bow-legged but very very satisfied! [Dv, #66]

> Leonne is a good choice if you want a quick fuck with a nice looking girl. Don't expect intimacy, GFE or a long stay, just a good hard shag. [Nobbin the Nob, #170]

Whilst recognizing the role of commercial sex in fulfilling a desire for intimacy, paying for sex is also about satisfying men's sexual 'needs'. This is commonly constructed around the categories of sexual pleasure and the erotic. But what, then, is meant by sexual pleasure and erotic performance?

Plummer (1975) describes pleasure as the interpretation of internal physiological changes that are 'triggered off' by some kind of external erotic stimulus. The erotic, he argues, is often 'tinged with meanings of "dirt and filth" ... "guilt and shame" ... "danger and excitement" [or] "power and assertiveness"' (Plummer, 1975, p.34). Although sexual pleasure is often described as a physiological response, it has also been described as more of an embodied emotional response, especially by women (Gavey, McPhillips and Braun, 1999). Thus, not only can pleasure and the erotic be ascribed various meanings but they are fundamentally gendered (Wilton, 1994) as well as constructed around other forms of social stratification such as class, age and ethnicity.

It can be argued that sex has no fundamental ontological value or reality beyond the symbolic terrain in which it takes place. For example, Oerton and Phoenix suggest that 'embodied, potentially erotic, intimate physical encounters do not exist in and of themselves' (2001, p.387). Indeed, they go further to argue that, 'in practice this means that the act of physically stimulating someone to the point of orgasm need not always be a sexual act' (p.408).

In this chapter we explore men's stories of pleasure and performance. First, we explore men's accounts of their sexual pleasure and their expectations of commercial sex; here we consider the role of the penis in constructions of masculinity. Second, we focus on men's accounts of women's pleasure and, returning to the concept of the con discussed in Chapter 4, we consider their accounts of female orgasm. In doing so, in this chapter we examine how men's accounts of sexual pleasure and erotic performance enable the management of a potentially deviant sexual identity.

Men's Pleasure and Women Pleasing Men

Men Defining Sexual Pleasure

Paying for sex threatens masculinity because it raises the question of why such men, as rhetoric goes, 'can't get it for free'. This is a view sometimes perpetuated by sex workers themselves. For example, in a study by Weatherall and Priestley, one woman states: 'he's paying so he's the victim (...) so he's the loser that can't get sex so he has to go to the person that's providing it' (2001, p.336). There is also limited evidence to suggest that some men visit sex workers because they are lonely or perceive themselves to be ugly or otherwise inadequate (see, for example, Campbell, 1998). *PunterNet*, however, offers a very different view of commercial sex. It does not depict paying for sex as the last resort for desperate men, but as a hobby – a choice that men make because paying for sex can be quick, cheap, convenient, and fun. In this sense, sites such as *PunterNet* construct and maintain the idea that both the women who sell sex and the men who pay for it are active agents in a commercial sexual transaction.

Not surprisingly, men's physical pleasure and satisfaction are central to the commercial encounter. On *PunterNet*, the vast majority – over 90 per cent – of sexual encounters are reviewed positively. Carol Queen (2000, pp.111-12), who was a sex worker for five years, suggests that masculinity can be played out in different ways and argues that 'male sexuality is often unduly performance oriented, even mechanized. The man often has to make all the moves. With a whore, he can lie back and receive'. On *PunterNet*, men tell stories that centre on their own pleasure. Echoing the perspective of Carol Queen, within the context of commercial sex, men's stories concentrate on the way in which sex workers are able, or not able, to please. The phrase 'she is keen to please' can often be found in men's *PunterNet* accounts, for example:

> she was keen to please and did all that i wanted, even performing again after a rest ... [Robbie, #203]

> I watched both girls together for a while then I had Anya whilst Lara sat on her face so that I could kiss those lovely tits of hers ... both ladies are a pleasure to be with and keen to please. [Nig2259@excite.com, #169]

However, the data suggest that a negative sexual experience is usually blamed on the sex worker, as the following account shows:

> Her technique is appalling, spend more time wanking than sucking, won't suck to completion, and struggled to please me at all. [Blowman, #30]

This view, which we shall explore in a little more detail below, is typical of men's accounts in that it supports the idea that sex workers are offering a service, and that specific standards of service are to be expected when money is exchanged. Commercial sex, thus, specifically entails paying for someone who is willing to please, for example:

> This versatile and accommodating lady will not be rushed, she will do almost anything to please her visitor ... [Altosax, #8]

PunterNet reinforces the view that paying for sex is a commercial transaction – nothing more – but that honesty and good service are vital. The view expressed above also allows men to place their own sexual desires at the fore in a way that may not be possible within consensual non-commercial heterosex. As McKeganey also found: 'By paying for sex the males felt able to place their own sexual desires at centre stage ...' (1994, p.295).

The Perfect Penis

Normative heterosex revolves around sexual intercourse, specifically, penis-to-vagina penetration. Thus, the penis and penile performance are central to the construction of male sexual identity. Indeed, it has been argued that analysis of sexual competence is crucial to any understanding of contemporary masculinity (Tiefer, 1995). Men's accounts of commercial sex devote considerable attention to describing the penis and discussing its performance. It is well documented that euphemistic language is characteristic of sex talk (Holland *et al.*, 1994) but particularly so with respect to this. The penis is referred to as a distinct entity, or 'a "self" with its own will' (Potts, 2001, p.145) and euphemistic comedic terms such as 'John Thomas', 'trouser snake', and 'old man' are used in addition to the more common 'cock', 'knob' and 'prick'. Previous research suggests that sometimes the penis is also referred to as a miniature male person (Lopate, 1994). The role of the penis in men's sex talk highlights the significance of a genital focus within men's sexuality. Nelson (1985) suggests that this focus is based on the idea of male sexuality as a technical performance requiring 'proper' erection and ejaculation.

Of central concern is the achievement and maintenance of a 'quality' erection. For example, one man writes:

> ... very sexy massage, her hand technique and the 'old man' was the best I have ever experienced – I don't think I have ever had a hard on as big! [Punterex, #191]

An especially large and a particularly hard penis is, thus, a sign of masculinity in good working order. However, within the context of *PunterNet* such penile discussion and display is not really directed at women but, as Diamond (1991) has pointed out, it is for the benefit of other men. The discussion of such magnificent erections constitutes a 'narcissistic reflection of conventional masculinity' (Kibby and Costello, 1999, p.358) and a declaration of normative heterosexual masculinity. The contemporary male sexual script, as Kimmel has identified:

> ... contains dicta for sexual distancing, objectification, phallocentrism, a pressure to become and remain erect without ejaculation for as long as possible, all of which serve as indicators of masculinity as well as sexual potency. Adequate sexual functioning is seen as the proof of masculinity (Kimmel, 1990, p.101).

Concurring with this Segal (1997) suggests that collectively, whether in locker rooms, in the workplace, or on the net, male sexual performance serves to consolidate and confirm masculinity. Men's shared experience of the penis, in particular, thus allows men to gain a sense of normative heterosexual masculine identity.

Previous research on consensual non-commercial sex suggests that coitus is the locus of normative heterosex and that the 'coital imperative' (Jackson, 1984, p.44) renders sex without coitus unthinkable. Such penetration, with (male) ejaculation is considered to be 'real', 'normal', sex but little is known about the meaning of sex within commercial encounters. Weatherall and Priestley (2001) suggest that a rich variety of constructions of sex exists within sex work although the coital imperative is reflected within the pricing structure of (street) work. However other accounts of commercial sex, including the data presented here, indicate that a range of sex acts are practiced and that if a hierarchy exists then coitus is not necessarily at the top of that hierarchy. For example, although 'ultimate', or 'full sex' – as coitus is often described – is more expensive than oral sex, it is usually less expensive than anal sex.

The inability to achieve or maintain erection is, therefore, problematic, and not solely in relation to commercial sex. For example, Morris suggests:

> It happens to nearly every man sometime during the life span. Mild-mannered Limp Penis refuses to transform into throbbing hard Superpenis. Perceived as no longer more powerful than a locomotive, most males who experience erection difficulties feel emasculated and ashamed (1997, p.121).

Arguably, this is particularly so during the commercial encounter, which is not only usually subject to clear time constraints, but its primary purpose is to achieve conventional male sexual gratification; that is, erection and ejaculation.

In men's accounts on *PunterNet*, erectile difficulties are often justified in relation to the man's nervousness and inexperience as a punter, once again serving to alleviate the potential attribution of personal inadequacy. For example:

Now this was my first time in any paying for sex activity and so I was a little wary to say the least. It took me a while to get hard. Infact she had to start sucking me off before I even started growing. [Billog, #28]

As I was very nervous (lst timer) it took a while to get a hard on. Meanwhile gave her a good oral session to get me hard. Eventually got a reasonable hard on and fucked her in doggy position (mine and sascha's favourite position). I'm glad I chose Sascha – she was very understanding about it being my 1st time. Hopefully next time I'll have a mega hard-on next time I visit her. [Rega3, #198]

Other explanations were also offered, for example:

After quite some time Katie progresses to the owo. Which was good. Nice use of the fingers on the old balls, and a very nice hand and mouth technique. However, we were having such a good chin wag whilst this was going on that the trouser snake forgot what he was there for. [Captainsoftware, #40]

In the study by Campbell (1998), which is based on 28 telephone interviews with men in the Liverpool area in the UK, some men reported that commercial sex relieved the pressure of performance and sexual achievement. For impotent men, commercial sex provided a safer environment within which they could deal with inadequate sexual performance. Of course the very concept of impotence is not unproblematic. Tiefer (1985), for example, argues that the increasing use of this term can be seen as part of the medicalising of sexuality, and suggests that since being a man depends on sexual adequacy, impotence becomes the problem of an individual man. However, impotence is not a word that appears in men's cyber accounts of commercial sex. As we have outlined, when faced with a penis that does not perform, men are resistant to the attribution of personal, individual inadequacy, preferring to apportion blame elsewhere.

Another concern discussed in men's accounts is failure to ejaculate. This was reported infrequently but, once again, this failure is justified in relation to external extenuating circumstances, such as tiredness or intoxication:

She informed me that we only had two minutes and suggested she finish me off by hand, but after a week long millenium celebration fuelled by alcohol and designer drugs it didn't happen. [Shyboy, #222]

She was very responsive and I like to think she enjoyed it also. Sad to say, at that time of night after a very long day, I only managed it once. Shame on me. Finished up talking for last half hour or so. [Ixion, #105]

Previous research highlights that the use of alcohol, or other drugs, is often used to defend otherwise unsatisfactory sexual performance (Rhodes, 1996; Rhodes and Cusick, 2002). Men's recourse to such a defense serves to highlight that under normal circumstances they would have no erectile dysfunction or difficulties with ejaculation.

It is clear that in their sexual stories, men do not blame themselves for the inability to ejaculate and when extenuating circumstances do not apply, the woman is blamed. In the following account, and after a failure to ejaculate, one man receives a refund:

> 2 mins asked if i wanted her on top no continued with oral she complained of jaw ache started to take rubber of for hand finish i asked for full sex mish then doggy to attempt to finish maid nocked after about 15 min's didnt come she was finished with me though got 50% refund poor poor service. [janothing, #10]

Although ejaculation failure in general was seldom discussed, failure to ejaculate a second time was more frequently reported. For example, one punter states:

> This time I didn't come so quickly – in fact Megan lapped at my bum for around 15 minutes before I felt too guilty that I wasn't coming and told her it wasn't going to work for me. [John Spencer, #117]

Much more common appears to be a concern with 'premature' ejaculation although, as Morris (1997) rightly identifies, there is no universal or definitive understanding of this. Premature ejaculation may be defined as the inability of a man to delay ejaculation before minimal sexual stimulation, for example, during foreplay or initial penis-vagina contact. It may also be defined in relation to partner expectation, which is likely to vary considerably. Within men's accounts, premature ejaculation is defined in relation to their own normative expectations of delay. Whilst punters view premature ejaculation as disappointing, they usually justify this within the context of the sex worker's overwhelming sensuality and/or skill. That is, she was just 'too good':

> this girl knows how to suck cock, and I came quickly. [Rimmer boy, #202]

> Tiffany's BBBJ is simply superb. She takes it deep and uses her tongue perfectly. The only problem is she is too damn good at it so I shot my load early on. [Billog, #28]

Sometimes this explanation was also given within the context of a first punting experience:

> first time with a working girl and i was very nervous. she was so lovely and it is so true her smile is exquisite. she gave slow oral leading to sex with her. i did not last long but it was my fault as she is so sensual. [Wally, #229]

Other men also expressed an awareness of this problem and described how they were able to prevent themselves from ejaculating prematurely:

> Nicole did (covered) oral on me, she lying on the floor, on her back, me kneeling, giving good quality head on Kim. I had to call a halt to this as I nearly "wasted" too early! ! [Dickking, #59]

After I had given oral to both ladies I asked them if they would use the double ended dildo. I didn't want to stop them from enjoying themselves with it but I needed a bj off both girls together so I put myself between them and I needn't of asked because they both obliged with a smile. I don't know how I stopped myself from coming too soon but the sight was very erotic indeed. [Nig2259, #169]

Men's own sexual satisfaction is clearly paramount. The failure to achieve or maintain an erection and failure to ejaculate, either once or more than once, are key concerns. So, whilst Carol Queen (2001) is, in part, correct to suggest that commercial sex offers men the opportunity to 'lie back and enjoy', paying for sex is still a performance of masculinity. Whilst we might expect men's accounts only to describe sexual prowess and success, it is interesting to note that this is not all they contain. Whether the accounts are true representations of real events, or not, they demonstrate an understanding and recognition of flawed performance. However, in these accounts, men's sexual flaws and failures are directly attributed to women, rather than to men themselves, either because women are 'too good' at their job, or not 'good enough'.

Men 'Giving' Women Pleasure

... And Women Enjoying 'It'

Integral to any definition or description of a good commercial experience is the tacit acceptance that women who sell sex must genuinely love their work. The following extracts illustrate this point:

Melanie is friendly, sexy, and, above all, clearly happy in her work. She radiates cheerfulness, making the whole experience intensely pleasurable. [Lancealot, #132]

Seemed to genuinely enjoy her work. [Samtheman, #212]

She certainly puts a lot into her work which is a pleasure. [Wiccan Wanderer, # 249]

Whilst some sex workers may enjoy selling sex – and others may not - no doubt, this approach serves to perpetuate and reinforce the concept of sex work as either normal sex or ordinary work, rather than as a form of abuse, as it is sometimes represented in the literature, and elsewhere. This is an important feature of the normative world constructed by *PunterNet*, since it is necessary to reinforce the idea of paying for sex as an acceptable hobby, rather than something shameful and which causes harm. Indeed, the construction and maintenance of men's identity within *PunterNet* depends on this.

Research on consensual non-commercial sex suggests that definitions of sex 'are focused on the notion of reciprocity, where sex involves giving (and receiving) pleasure' (McPhillips, Braun and Gavey, 1991, p.235). Although men's accounts focus considerably on their own pleasure, there is significant, if not equal discussion of the pleasure which they believe they give to women. However, this is not necessarily universal across the whole sex industry; it is much more likely to apply to indoor, rather than outdoor, workers for example (Lever and Dolnick, 2000). Accounts of non-commercial heterosex suggest that behaviours are highly patterned. Drawing on script theories, some authors suggest a prescribed sequence of events. Gagnon and Simon describe this as:

> Kissing, tongue kissing, manual and oral caressing of the body, particularly the female breasts, manual and oral contacts with both the female and male genitalia, usually in this sequence, followed by intercourse in a number of positions (Gagnon and Simon, 1987, p.2).

Men's accounts show striking similarities with the sexual script outlined above, for example:

> During the session Racquel kisses (with tongues) and cuddles, she also appears to enjoy receiving oral. Her oral (with) is exceptional and very gentle, she kissed and nibbled my balls then liked and sucked my cock taking it deep into her mouth. The sex to completion (her on top) was also excellent. [Alan, #6]

Men's sexual stories show that giving pleasure – usually in the form of cunnilingus, masturbation, and sometimes penis-to-vagina intercourse – is important to them. However, this should not necessarily be seen as an altruistic deed, but as another way in which men establish that they are good at sex; that is, women's pleasure serves as an indicator of men's sexual performance. Some men suggest that the sex worker should be thanking them, for example:

> I went back down for some more oral while my cock recovered and that's when she forgot the clock altogether. i like to eat pussy, and she had no intention of hurrying me up. after what seem an eternity she repaid my handy (sorry tonguing) work with a bj to top all bj's. i think it was her way of saying thank you. [Baron, #16]

Indeed, one individual believed that it was he who should receive payment:

> ... she starts licking my balls and all along my very stiff cock licking the end like a lollipop finally sucking down on me hard she seems to love sucking cock ... now I'm ready to have that wet pussy and is she wet, her legs hook around my neck and do I ram her hard, she is really thrusting me hard now pleading for more maybe she should pay me for the pleasure I am giving her. [Bigjohnuk, #25]

There is considerable debate in the literature on sex work as to whether women enjoy sex when it is in exchange for money. There is only some limited evidence to suggest that women do enjoy sex work. Brewis and Linstead, for example, use the term 'heaven trade' to describe 'clients whom the worker finds irresistibly attractive' (2000, p.220). This implies that there may be a hierarchy of punters ranging from the sexually attractive, to the average, to the downright rebarbative. Edwards (1993, p.99), however, argues that: 'Contrary to an archetypal belief about prostitute women, there is little job satisfaction'. This is supported by the work of Perkins and Bennett (1985) who argue that women who sell sex rarely experience any real sexual excitement in the course of their work. The previously published literature is, thus, fairly confused on this point. Rarely did we come across an account in which a man did *not* believe that the sex worker had enjoyed the sexual experience, as the following extracts illustrate:

> Diane is an enthusiastic fucker and puts a lot into it. Then it was something new for me, Anal. Diane really seems to enjoy this... [Bowmore, #34]

> More kissing was followed by me going down on her which she seemed to enjoy ... [DelBoy, #57]

> Not wishing to disclose too many personal details – but suffice to say Paula's speciality is her 'A' level, where I believe she passed with honours, and as I've already said I'm a 'bum' man, and so this was a great experience. An added bonus was that Paula seemed to really enjoy that part too. [Fireblade, #73]

> After this she then laid back on the bed allowing me proceed to give her a blow job and she also prompted me to finger her at the same time. She certainly sounded like she was enjoying things at this stage. [Jay, #109]

So, whilst it is not clear whether women who sell sex do experience any pleasure, it is clear that the men who pay for sex describe that they do.

In completing a field report on *PunterNet* men are asked to state whether they would recommend a particular woman to other men. If men believe that a sex worker enjoys sex then they seem much more likely to recommend her to others, as the following extract shows:

> 36a – excellent breasts – she seemed to enjoy them being sucked ... I would definitely recommend her. [Jazzer, #110]

Both historically and within contemporary popular mythology, it is assumed that men 'give' women pleasure and that women are the passive – and grateful – recipients of this. When women appear unresponsive – in spite of their best efforts – once again, men do not take responsibility and the blame is laid firmly at her feet rather than his:

> [She] seemed rather nervous and immature ... Not very interested or responsive either ... Needs to get more interested and responsive. [Randydoc, #195]

> Toy show was not erotic, her covered BJ was useful, her bum was producing an unpleasant smell. I lost all my drive and erection ... In summary she was doing it all by the numbers with no hint of enjoyment. [Horny Devil, #97]

Women's Orgasm

Béjin (1986) has put forward the idea of an 'orgasmic imperative', arguing that it is a pervasive feature of modern western societies. That is, orgasm has come to be seen as a 'normal', 'natural', 'healthy' and expected constituent of sexual experience. According to Nicholson (1993), this imperative has come to symbolize sexual competence, and has been (re)produced in sexological, therapeutic and some feminist discourses, amongst others. Being 'good' at sex means having an orgasm and, in the case of men, being able to 'give' women an orgasm. The orgasmic imperative is also evident in everyday discourse, for example, Tavella states:

> Men have become very concerned about this lately, always asking 'Did you? Did you come?' (Tavella, 1992, p.2).

Moreover, Potts (2000), drawing on the work of Foucault (1978), suggests that if we think of ourselves as being our sex, 'then it follows that orgasm is not merely a celebration of who we are, it is our ultimate meeting with our true (sexual) selves ... and the most privileged site of "access" to the self of the other' (Potts, 2000, p.59).

Roberts *et al.*, (1995) suggest that men's sexual narratives are dominated by stories of 'technique and work', or practices which men apply to women's passive bodies. Of particular significance here is the belief in men's ability to 'give', or 'provide' women with orgasm. Ehrenreich, Hess and Jacobs (1986) suggest that this can be attributed directly to feminist influenced sexology which encouraged men to think about women's 'needs' as well as their own. This, according to Braun, Gavey and McPhillips, (2003), has been supported by marital sex advice given from the 1920s onwards and can be seen in the guidance books on this subject. The concept of reciprocity is also supported by our data and the way in which men describe themselves as sensitive or considerate when they set out to put the sex worker's pleasure before their own, for example:

> Why don't more chaps ask if the girl would like to come first? It's much more fun! At least offer! [2xanite, #2]

Men particularly like to be commended for their efforts, as this extract shows:

> She complemented me for being considerate and I obliged by making sure she enjoyed the experience as much as I did. [Tummyboy, #235]

However, as Roberts *et al.*, (1995, p.526) argue, central to this is not women's pleasure *per se* but that: 'Giving women an orgasm is a demonstration of the man's sexual capacities and skill'. Within the context of commercial sex, we would go further and argue that since paying for sex threatens the maintenance of sexual identity, it does not just prove the quality of men's technique, but it also reaffirms men's hegemonic, heterosexual masculine identities. Concurring with this, and in a critique of early sexology, Jeffreys argues:

The woman in sexual intercourse must not just be penetrated, but be swept away in a delicious submission to the will of her master and mate. The experience of female orgasm was supposed to signify and effect the woman's subjection (1997, p.228).

Men's accounts of giving women pleasure are dominated by discussion of women's orgasm, as the following extracts indicate:

Her pussy tasted sweet, and I could tell she was enjoying herself, as I licked her her hand came down to spread her lips and tease her clit, her moans got louder and she tensed up, I tasted her juices as she reached her climax, her fingers had gone White whilst gripping the bed as she came. [Slappy, #226]

In fact, men spend much more time writing about this than they do writing about their own experience of orgasm, which is often just described as 'the inevitable', and left at that.

Dominant in the literature on orgasm is discussion of the 'coital imperative' as the means through which 'proper' female orgasm is achieved (Gavey, McPhillips and Braun, 1999). Whilst the limited research on this subject suggests that many women do not actually orgasm during penis-vagina penetration, it does appear to be a normative expectation. Moreover, Nicolson and Burr suggest that, 'the most favoured experience is mutual orgasm *during* intercourse' (2003, p.1740). This is exemplified in the following extract:

Nicole [was] riding me with her own wonderful brand of movement, culminating in an explosive orgasm, me slightly later than Nicole. [Dickking, #59]

Men's sexual stories echo these normative expectations; in that most of the *PunterNet* accounts describe women's orgasm as occurring within the confines of penis-vagina intercourse:

More kissing and cuddling before she put condom on me and had sex in several positions. She was on top and she also orgasmed. [Tummyboy, #235]

a fantastic clit which she loved me licking and asked for more. I'm not sure if she came at this stage ... I moved up and took her (mish) and the whole place must have heard the noises she made. Her face was amazing. This girl loves sex and shows it. [Xizzy, #242]

However, a smaller number of men do describe 'giving' women an orgasm during oral sex, for example:

Instead of touching her I offered to go down on her and she replied 'Oh yes baby, make me cum'. [Shyboy, #222]

Men's accounts of sexual pleasure are generally consistent with what is known about this within a non-commercial context. That is, whilst women frequently report faking orgasm, the majority of men do not believe themselves to have encountered a faker (Holland *et al.*, 1998; Roberts *et al.*, 1995); this is something that happens to other men. In spite of this, considerable attention is given within men's accounts, to establishing the genuineness of orgasm. Analysis of the data shows that reference is frequently made to the seemingly verifiable signs of orgasm, which are often described in considerable detail. For example, making a noise was considered to be a reasonably reliable measure of orgasm:

> ... she started to ride my (covered) cock she just went wild. I am sure she came from the noises she was making. [Sj, #225]

> I must have spent a good 10 mins down there. She made all the right noises and I think she definitely orgasmed. [Bob, #31]

Men also commented on the amount of lubrication women produced, believing that copious lubrication was a sure sign of female orgasm, and even multiple orgasm:

> she brought herself off on my cock with a shuddering orgasm, I could see the juices coming out of her pussy. [Johnathon, #118]

> She is extremely Multi-Orgasmic going by the amount of juices she secreets. [Scooby-Doo1, #214]

In a far smaller number of instances, men described sexual flushes as evidence:

> I slipped on the rubber jacket and entered her very, very tight tunnel – missionary style and I saw something I have never seen with a lady – she came in about 4 strokes. No fake her upper chest flushed to prove it – I think she was as surprised as me. [Wildwilly2, #246]

Men's accounts illustrate how they draw on traditionally held ideas about an inborn and universal biological sexual mechanism and the concept, put forward by Masters and Johnson, of a sexual response cycle (Tiefer, 1995). Implicit in this too, is the idea that there may be something wrong with women if they do not have orgasms (Nicolson and Burr, 2003).

Previous research shows that sex workers commonly fake orgasm for the clients' benefit. For example, Charlotte, a London sex worker, states; 'The men really want to believe that you fancy them. They love it when you make a lot of noise. They really kid themselves that you're enjoying it' (in Salvadori, 1997, p.120). And sex worker Barbara writes: 'The worse ones [punters] are the ones who don't turn you on and think that all women have to have about six orgasms before they will penetrate them' (in Bishop and Robinson, 1998, p.234). But, one of the men in our study believed that certain signs could not be faked:

> She really likes her job and when we got on with sex she really enjoyed it. Certain things a woman cant fake no matter how hard they try! [Tummyboy, #235]

Another man was less certain and illustrated the ambiguity felt by many men. Whilst they do not believe that they have encountered a faker they are open to the idea that they can never be absolutely sure:

> We then progressed to me pleasuring her..., which I enjoyed (and I hope she did, although you can never really tell for certain). [Captainsoftware, #40]

Faking orgasm generates anxiety for both men and women (Roberts *et al.*, 1995). Commercial sex is not only about men's pleasure but about men giving pleasure to women. However, just as non-commercial heterosex revolves around the idea of sex as a 'mutual event' (Braun, Gavey and McPhillips, 2003) so, too, does commercial sex. When men pay for sex they are also paying for a sexual performance – real or otherwise – in which their sexual prowess is affirmed through the sex workers own pleasure and orgasm. As Nicolson and Burr note, the orgasmic imperative, predominantly through coitus, ensures that women are responsible for ensuring that men experience themselves as good lovers and 'if the woman fails to enjoy sex, then she is somehow to blame, because if she were not, it would suggest male sexual inadequacy' (2003, p.1737).

We must revisit here the concept of 'the con' (Maurer, 1940; Goffman, 1952) since anybody reading these accounts, as we did, would surely believe that the notion of female orgasm in sex work is the biggest con of all. In the context of non-commercial heterosex, the literature suggests that the majority of women have faked orgasm. Even though the majority of men are aware of such a con – the same literature suggests that men are unlikely to believe that they have been conned in this way. Our data show that men expect women who sell sex to enjoy it – this implies that she is good at her job – and probably means that clients are more likely to return. In relation to the construction of male sexual identity, women's orgasm is an affirmation of male potency and technique, serving to destigmatize those who pay for sex. Sex workers, thus, have an obvious interest in displaying sexual pleasure and perpetuating the notion of orgasm in sex work. Whilst not excluding the possibility that some sex workers may find pleasure in their work, our data illustrate how commercial sexual relations perpetuate a con game *par excellence*.

Reciprocity, Identity and the Gift of Pleasure

So, what does this tell us about the ways in which men manage deviant identities? The very fact that many men are sharing their sexual stories of commercial sex, often for the first time, might mean that they have discovered a sympathetic community. This community may simultaneously both serve to strengthen and destigmatize their identity as a punter, as well as normalize their behaviour.

Men who pay for sex are labelled as sad, bad or mad and these labels can be juxtaposed with representations of sex workers. First, we have the 'tarts with the hearts' who fulfill some deep emotional need for intimacy. Second, the 'calculating whores' who are 'in it just for the money' (O'Connell Davidson, 1995; 1998). The men who visit such women must be sad (or mad) because it is clear, to others at least, that they are deluding themselves and unable to get '"it" for free'. Lastly, we have a depiction of the prostitute as used and abused, as Pederson and Hegna state:

> The popular image of the prostitute is the adult woman suffering from drug addiction, dressed in a short skirt and tall boots, working in the dark streets of big cities ... Traditional descriptions, scientific or popular, of the female prostitute have often depicted her as a victim (Pederson and Hegna, 2003, p.135).

She is drugged, beaten, possibly trafficked and enslaved. The men who use such prostitutes are bad or mad, or both.

Men's sexual stories focus on their own pleasure and the pleasure that they give to women. We argue that these accounts serve to challenge the view of men who pay for sex as sad, mad or bad and play a role in the management of this deviant identity. The punter feels pleasure because the sex worker exists to please him. If he fails to erect or achieve ejaculation then he is never to blame and if he 'comes too quickly' then she is to blame. However, the punter is paying for her pleasure as well as his own. When the sex worker feels pleasure, his technique and prowess are accountable but when she does not 'perform' to his satisfaction, then it is because she is 'frigid', or simply, 'bad at her job'. In the same way that non-commercial heterosex involves giving and receiving, commercial sex not only centres on the idea that sex workers should please men but that the punter should give pleasure too.

Vance (1984) suggests that men's concern with reciprocity may demarcate a more egalitarian type of sexual standards. However, such gifting is gendered and unequal, as Gilfoyle, Wilson and Brown note:

> ... women are seen as the object who is both 'given away' and 'given to'; while men, on the other hand, are seen as the subject, maintaining their dominance by both being the recipient of the woman and conferring on the object (woman) the gift of pleasure or orgasm (Gilfoyle, Wilson and Brown, 1992, p.218).

Lever and Dolnick (2000) suggest that, within commercial sex, men and women are complicit in the sexual performance of mutual pleasure; or rather, they agree to pretend. Our data suggest that the opposite is true. Whilst some punters have a healthy scepticism, the majority of men appear to believe that this pretence does not apply to them. To not believe that this is so would undermine the perceived certainties of paying for sex which is not only that sex workers are women who will have sex with them but that they should, and will, enjoy it.

Chapter 6

Doing the Business

Sex, Power and Agency

Implicit or explicit in most accounts of sex work is the desire to understand issues of power and agency; that is: who is in control – sex workers – or the men who pay for sex? In Chapter 1 we outlined some of the main positions adopted in response to this question and argued that various approaches exist, all of which position themselves differently on the continuum of sex/work/abuse. We adopt the position that sex work is essentially a business transaction, and not just because the primary reason for sex work is an economic one, but because this is reinforced by the language of the sex industry, which is one of trade. For example, sex workers refer to themselves as 'workers', 'working girls', 'professionals' and so on and they describe the sale of sex as a 'job' or the 'business' (Perkins and Bennett, 1985). We acknowledge that some forms of sex work may be brutal, harrowing and violent but maintain that such a universal position on sex work is untenable. Indeed, previous research suggests that the violence perpetrated against sex workers is most likely committed by a small number of men who are frequently violent. We echo the view advanced by Wood (2000) who argues that power needs to be understood as a contested and negotiated resource, enacted through interaction.

Men, too, describe sex work as a business exchange. This chapter examines men's accounts of sexual interaction, focusing specifically on the commercial nature of paying for sex. We begin by examining sex work within the context of leisure and consumer culture, exploring men's power as purchasers of sexual services. We then consider the concept of value-for-money – an important feature of men's experiences – and revisit some of the themes we discussed in earlier chapters. Finally, we explore men's experiences of time and temporality, and consider their accounts of time management in paid-for sex.

Leisure, Sex and Consumption

Many theorists concur on the importance of consumption for understanding the construction of identities within modern western societies. Indeed, many would place consumption at the very locus of identity. Writers have also suggested that emotional hedonism has become the driving force of consumption, whereby pleasure has become commodified. Extending this further Featherstone, suggests: 'As free time and leisure activities also became drawn into the orbit of the market, hobbies, pastimes and experiences come to increasingly depend upon the purchase of commodities' (1982, p.172). Writing specifically about sex work, Brewis and Linstead argue:

> The way in which leisure has come to play an important role in modern life, as a deserved respite from work, the positioning of the quest for pleasure as a crucial aspect of this free time, and the transformation of consumption from an activity carried out for sustenance alone into an activity which is seen to afford pleasure are, therefore, all important in the recognition of prostitution as a consumer industry in late Western modernity (Brewis and Linstead, 2000, p.209).

Although for sex workers the business of selling sex is a financial one, for men paying for sex is a leisure activity. The *PunterNet* site encourages men to think about sex as a form of leisure. Paying for sex is described variously as a hobby, a sport and a pass-time, as one respondent highlights:

> As an infrequent hobbyist I had one of those days where I felt the urge. [Captainsoftware, #40]

Sex is also seen as a reward for a hard day's labour, for example:

> Reading the reviews of Lucy (and having a tough meeting go very, very well) convinced me to dip in to the reserves ... Next time I'm in London, I'll allocate more funds for this sport and spend it all on her! [Lightfoot, #136]

According to Strasser (2003) commodification refers to the commercialisation of something that is not, by nature, commercial. This, she argues, is problematic in that the definition of the 'commercial' is both historically defined and socially constructed. The commodification of sex is problematic in that sex is traditionally defined as something that is not, by 'nature' commercial. It is something that should be freely given (or taken) and for women, in particular, supposedly imbued with feelings of love and romance.

Commercial sex is, and always has been, a commodity and the men who pay for sex are free to purchase this service whenever, and from whomever, they please. Men, thus, have purchasing power which can place them in a dominant position within the sex industry. They are explicit about their purchasing power – a man who goes away happy is one that will come back again (and again):

> Oh Morgan you have a lovely touch. I ... gained entry and Morgan rode me in a squatting position, and finally I took her on the bed-end with her legs fully wrapped around my neck. That was it!! I have been with Morgan before and I will be back again. [Saunaman, #213]

An unhappy man is unlikely to visit the same woman twice and will look elsewhere the next time he is looking to pay for sex:

... simply the worst experience I have had in a long long time and I personally wouldn't send my worst enemy their. She told me I could cum on her breasts and then moaned at how messy it was! The only consolation was that she dropped the dirty dripping tissues right in her lap and had to run off and wash! A fitting end to an awful experience. Avoid like the plague! Recommended: No. Would You Return: No. [Big Guy 58, #27]

... would advise anybody thinking about it to forget it – probably the worst woman I have been with and will remember this night for a long time for all the wrong reasons. Recommended: No. Would You Return: No. [Crikey, #49]

Chapters 1 and 2 in this book considered whether the virtual environment of *PunterNet.com* was serving to transform social relationships. The following extracts provide examples of the way in which *PunterNet* is transforming and enhancing men's purchasing power, not just as individuals, but as a social group:

Perhaps PunterNet will educate us a little more, and people like Debbie will either change her attitude (and learn a technique or two) or lose her clientele. I would certainly not recommend a visit. [Ltb, #140]

I am not a regular punter but have been viewing 'PunterNet' for a while and chose Selina because she visited your home and those field reports totally sold me on her but I did not know how true they were. [Expresstrain, #71]

As individual purchasers of sex, men are clearly free to exercise consumer choice. However, as we have argued elsewhere (Sharp and Earle, 2003), websites such as *PunterNet* create a virtual world in which men can exchange information and, arguably, become more demanding consumers.

Value-for-Money

It is clear from the accounts posted on *PunterNet* that men recognize paying for sex to be a largely commercial transaction; the language adopted by men is one of trade. Women are the sellers, and men, the buyers. As with any such transaction there is a concern with quality, quantity and price. As outlined in Chapter 3, sex can be sold either by the act or by the hour. Parlours and other establishments seem equally likely to offer sex either way whereas women working as escorts are much more likely only to offer their services by the hour. It could be argued that there is a clear hierarchy with escorts selling their time and other women selling their bodies, or access to specific body parts (for example, vaginas, hands, breasts and so on). As we describe in Chapter 3, the indoor sex industry is clearly stratified. In terms of value-for-money – or VFM – the walk-up, which is predominantly to be found in the Soho area of London is usually the cheapest. Appointments are not necessary, though usually only one woman is available at any one time, sometimes up to three women may be working. Massage parlours will often have several women working in a number of rooms. The parlours are run by a receptionist – who answers the phone, receives punters, and so on. In parlours, the owners usually take a percentage of the women's income. Appointments are not usually necessary although some do run appointment systems, and prices are variable. Other women work from premises, either on their own or with other women. Many premises will have a maid who serves a similar function to that of the receptionist within a parlour. Premises usually operate an appointment system and prices vary. Escorts work independently but usually charge the highest rates by the hour. They work on both an incall basis – where they will receive punters at their own premises – or an outcall basis – where they will visit the punter at a location such as a hotel.

Many men, although by no means all, express a concern with the VFM of each sexual encounter. A verdict of good VFM is equally likely to be used by men who spend a considerable amount of money, as it is by those who are spending comparatively little. For example, *Nelson* spent £200, whereas *Arroganza* only £40:

> Sex is very good and she has lots of energy. She will also play with herself standing over you so that you can watch. All in all this is one fun girl who is great to be with and very good value for money. [Nelson, #166]

> I said that I wanted everything, to which she replied '1 do anything except kissing'. I must have looked surprised as she then said '... and that means you can fuck me in the ass and cum on my face ... if you want!' All this for £40 ... BARGAIN! [Arroganza, #12]

The concept of VFM was also equally likely to be articulated by men expressing their satisfaction as by those expressing dissatisfaction, or a mixture of both. For example:

> All in all an absolutely wonderful experience and one of the best bbbj's I've had for a long time. Definitely worth the money. [Bob, #31]

> Reasonable massage, with no oil or talc. Lots of chat and good humour. Offered the goodies and I chose the lot. Great value at £40. She does oral with, didn't ask if she did BBBJ and then we had pleasant (no more than that) sex, mish and doggie while she played with my danglie bits. Big disappointment is that she doesn't kiss. All in all, good value and a really nice lady. [Jings Crivvens, #114]

> Over the phone, she said that prices were from 30-60, however, when I entered the room that the 'most she does' is breast relief, and that was £60. Yes, I should have made an excuse and left – certainly not VFM – more fool me! [Ltb, #140]

Quite what constitutes VFM is unique to each individual. It is certainly not just related to cost relative to time or sex act, but must also be understood in relation to some of the themes we have addressed in previous chapters: the surroundings in which sex takes place, their objectification and evaluation of women's bodies, and the commodification of women's emotion and identity. We shall briefly revisit some of these themes below.

Place

As we have discussed in previous chapters, place and environment are important features of men's experiences of commercial sex. Discussions of place, environment and ambience also feature frequently in men's accounts of VFM. A smart décor may remove some of the general stigma and sleaze associated with commercial sex. Public portrayal of commercial sex is often sleazy; sex workers are portrayed as unclean and punters as inadequate (Pheterson, 1993; Scambler and Scambler, 1997; Pederson and Hegna, 2003). For example:

> Inside was a little on the dingy side (reminded me of my student days) but on the whole fairly clean....a nice down to earth girl who is the genuine article, don't be put off by the surroundings ... On the whole good VFM. [Azure Knight, #14]

> all in all not a terrible experience, but the quality of what was on offer was shabby in terms of the surroundings, and the girls were far from top of the range. [Badboy, #15]

As we have outlined above, the indoor sex market is clearly demarcated in terms of place, price and what can be expected in terms of quality and service provision. This demarcation also relates to VFM. As one punter describes:

> Certainly one of the best appointed places I have visited. Nice, clean lounge with HUGE bar. Bedroom with massive bed big enough for 10 people! All in all, the best value I have EVER had! [Sj, #225]

Women working as escorts or from the more luxurious premises are usually more expensive, but they do not always offer the best VFM. However, walk-ups, which have the reputation for quick, cheap service, are often seen as a 'rip off'. In one account, *Sing*, describes his experience of walk-ups:

> Typical walk up room, perhaps a bit more smelly. Very rushed and cold, french was short and mostly hands, sex was me on top only, more money for other positions. Very poor VFM - I just read another FR about Denise, seems to be this address – wish I'd seen it first!! [Sing, #224]

However, another punter describes a more positive walk-up experience:

> It was on the first floor of the first walk up on the right in Moor Street approached from Cambridge Circus. The entrance is not discreet at all but felt safe. The room was functional but clean. ... somewhere from the depths of my recollection I recalled reading a series of FRs written by Anthony which left me the impression that walk ups were not the rip off places that I had hitherto imagined. Despite my initial reservations, I found it a satisfying experience - I normally prefer luxurious parlours and girlfriend type sex which are sadly thin on the ground in the London area. For £25, this appeared to me to be wonderful value for money as I've often paid up to 3 times this amount for a no better level of service in parlours elsewhere in the South East. At this price, I can see me visiting a few more walk ups in the near future. [Confuscius, #48]

Convenience is another important factor in evaluating VFM and strongly correlates to the stratification of the indoor sex market we have outlined above. Parlours, for example, are unlikely to have an appointment system and most of the punters included in the study consider this to be extremely favourable:

> Reasonable VFM. It does have the advantage of appointment not necessary once you know where to go. Let's face it I have had a lot worse for a lot more money! [W.H. Oami, #252]

Writing about the convenience of paying for sex, Queen writes:

> ... men see prostitutes because they can. The sex industry exists to get guys laid. Client's who've figured out how to work the system (who've learned where sex workers are, how to contact tem, and how to relate effectively to them) know that sex can be scheduled and arranged almost as easily as ordering takeout. (Queen, 2000, pp.108-9)

The indoor sex industry – particularly the parlour sector – is clearly quite competitive and VFM can play an important part in determining repeat business. For example:

> Until recently Lindsey was the best girl I'd visited by a mile, but in the last couple of months I've had great times in Yate and Weston SM which were better VFM on the whole. However I still think Lindesy is the best around the Heathrow area. [Tommo, #230]

> I don't think I would go again because I have had much better at other places. Having said that I have had much worse too. The georgian seems to be going downhill a little lately with its choice of girls (there are some real miserable looking ones) I will try to go elsewhere in future. [Assman, #13]

The data suggest that regular punters come to know what is reasonable and what is not in terms of good VFM. Their accounts also show that punting in some geographical areas is more expensive than in others. London is generally recognized as more expensive in comparison to other places – especially in terms of VFM, but comparisons between other town and cities are also made:

> Jezebel advertises her basic services starting £30 and going up to £70 which is slightly higher than the Aberdeen average. [Rough Neck, #207]

Identity and Emotion

In her discussion of emotional labour, Chapkis argues that one objection to the conferring of a work status to the sale of sex arises from the view that 'sexuality cannot be separated from the person of the prostitute' and, by implication, that emotion and identity, in themselves, cannot be commodified (1997, p.71). However, as Hochschild (1983) rightly argues, work that is considered to be 'women's work' is, in fact, often characterized by the commercialisation of emotion.

Our analysis of men's accounts show that punters often want to talk and 'get to know' sex workers and, moreover, that this is important to their satisfaction and their evaluation of VFM. For example, *Antonym* states:

That first meeting was so out of the ordinary, exciting and enjoyable that I've just celebrated my tenth visit to this incredible lady. That fact alone testifies that Jaynah is utterly fascinating and delightful. Those of you who venture beyond the Field Reports page and read her postings on the board will know that she is intelligent, versatile, wise and witty. She is all that and more as an escort. Those of you who have not managed to drag yourselves away from the FR's [field reports] may have read the 'blow by blow' accounts submitted by others. Whilst accurate, they do little justice to Jaynah's character, commitment and expertise ... Take time to get to know Jaynah properly both before and during your visit. [Antonym, #11]

I found Anna very pleasent to talk to as she gave me a very sensual massage with oil, rubbing oil on her tits and then massaging me with her tits. [Boff, #32]

In another account *Cfothar* stresses the importance of sex workers being able to 'engage' with punters:

If you are in the mood for good simple straight action this would be a good value choice – but if like me you need more to get your jaded appetite whetted you probably need someone with more engagement ... [Cfothar, #42]

And other punters clearly differentiate between women who appear to be engaging and responding and those who do not. Whilst the quality of the action and their evaluation of women's bodies are both important, successful sex workers (as defined by men), are those who show willing:

Great fun and great value for money. She seems genuinely to enjoy her work. Will see her again. For anyone that punts on a regular basis (and for many that don't) Mellissa should be on your 'must- do list'. [Kerravon, #126]

Jane is full of energy and enthusiasm ... All in all this is one fun girl who is great to be with and very good value for money. [Nelson, #166]

Women who do not show enthusiasm tend to get negative reviews and are judged to offer poor value, for example:

Spent ages drinking some tea she'd made me, and seemed very hesitant about undressing. Not very interested or responsive either. Doesn't kiss, even though I'd asked Choice and been told she did. Tight pussy but not good value. Needs to get more interested and responsive. [Randydoc, #195]

In terms of VFM, emotional labour certainly has exchange value. However, not all topics of conversation are equally valued. As we discussed in Chapter 3, men often find evidence of maternity and maternal identity distasteful. So, any discussion of children and boyfriends, for example, was unwanted:

> Friendly and chatty, mainly about her boyfriend, or pimp, not exactly a turn-on . I definitely didn't leave with a smile, complete waste of money when there are so many advertising ... [Reuters, #199]

> Nice chat for around 45 mins, although it was a touch off-putting when she started talking about her kids. [BJ Friend, #29]

O'Connell Davidson (1996) suggests that during sexual encounters the sex worker becomes 'socially dead' in that 'her real identity and personal history is invariably concealed from the client, who has no real interest in it'. In Chapter 3 we discussed men's objectification of women's bodies, the value they placed on youth and their dislike of maternal bodies. We would argue that this is not solely based on aesthetic judgement but on a general dislike of being reminded of women's private, sexual and/or maternal identity. That is, in discussing sexual partners the punter is reminded that she is only having sex with him for money and in discussing children, the punter is aware of the sex worker as 'mother'. This may disrupt his notion of a 'figure of motherhood' in which: 'The "good mother" is self-sacrificing, selfless and probably not seen as sexual' (Woodward, 2003, p.26) and, thus, blurs the culturally accepted dichotomy between mother/whore.

It may also be true that in paying for sex, the punter also become 'socially dead' in that he may prefer his personal biography and identity to remain private:

> Got in the room and had a shower, then Tia laid me face down on the bed and started massaging my back and chatting a bit, Tia asked me if i had a girlfriend? like i need reminding of my other half at a time like that. [Ugly Bastard]

Thus, whilst some aspects of the sex worker's identity may be concealed from men within a usually tacit form of agreement between sex worker and client, the sale of sex is only defined as value-for-money when women appear to be genuinely offering something of themselves. As Wilton argues, sex work takes much of its meaning from its position, 'in relation to the emotion/commerce boundary [being] positioned firmly on the "emotion" side' (1999, p.187). In spite of a general concern with VFM, the irony is that the notion that sex workers do it just for the money is unthinkable to some. As *Martinkute* states:

> Very reluctant to participate in anything other than straight sex. Gave – half-hearted covered blowjob only. Doesn't encourage any touching and to be honest the sex was below average, because she just lays there. A pity as she could become very popular if she wanted. I'm afraid she just wants your money ... [Martinkute, #147]

Bodies, Youth and Experience

Descriptions of women's physicality feature heavily in men's accounts of paying for sex and can form part of their evaluation of whether a transaction is considered VFM. For example, within a culture which equates youth with desirability (Featherstone, 1982), older women can command less than younger women, hence older women are often better 'value', as *Rammie* states:

> We then kissed and chatted for the rest of the hour even though she had another customer waiting. In summary; excellent value for money in terms of time and the unlimited choice of sex acts. If you can think of it Sandy will do it! However, her well worn look and IMHO [in my humble opinion] slightly phoney personality will not suit everyone. A young provider would undoubtedly charge more for this level of service. As they say you get what you pay for! [Rammie, #194]

Men's accounts also sometimes equate youth with inexperience, and older women with experience and better technique, as *Desperate Dan*, describes:

> ... I find that older women are much better at sex than the young girls ... All in all quite satisfying. [Desperate Dan, #58]

Interestingly, we feel that men who pay for sex with older or more 'mature' women, need to justify their choices, as though this somehow perverted cultural norms and the association of sex with youth and desire. This cultural norm, we suggest, exists both within the wider social world, and within the social world of *PunterNet.com*:

> She's 'blonde' mid 40s, full bodied (her words), busty and has a lovely smile. If you're looking for a 19 year old dolly bird, forget it. But if you want someone who knows her stuff, she's the one. [Beardyone, #18]

> If you are after an 18 year old with rock hard boobs then don't bother. If you are looking for a REAL woman with maturity, a sense of humour, and a real feeling for what turns a man on, then Chelsea is for you. Would I return? Try and keep me away. [Drummer, #65]

Given the wide ranging literature that focuses on the objectification of women's bodies and the centrality placed on this in relation to sex work, it is surprising to note the women's physicality – whilst present – was not a core feature of VFM. Our analysis of the data indicates that the commodification of emotion was far more important. Evaluation of VFM was also connected to place and the expectations associated with the different locations in which sex is for sale.

The Temporality of Paying for Sex

Time is often represented as an objective and *a priori* category (Grosz, 1993; 1999). However, many commentators have been critical of this representation suggesting that the unidirectional, taken-for-granted nature of time is not a fact but a socially constructed ideal (Adam, 1990; Davies, 1996). By focusing on time we are able to explore further the locus of power in the sex industry. We have argued that selling sex is a financial exchange; but sex workers do business whereas men are indulging a hobby. The temporal organization of sex work is, thus, very different for these two parties.

Brewis and Linstead (2000) suggest that women's sex work is influenced by their life-cycle and the life-cycle of others (for example, their children's). They suggest:

> Time here is not pure, but complex, contaminated, even reversible and the ways in which the interactants experiences and interpret time emphasize the complexity of identity work ... (Brewis and Linstead, 2000, p.273).

As other researchers have also identified, for sex workers, time is work time and it is carefully managed to maximize income. Sex workers are also affected by the passage of natural time in that there are busy, and less busy, periods. *PunterNet* advises men to be wary of busy times, such as the lunch hour and early afternoon and what they describe as the 'evening rush' after 7 o'clock – especially in parlours. Previous research describes the way in which sex workers need to manage experiences of boredom or what has been called the 'tedious downtime' (Brewis and Linstead, 2000) during these quiet, yet unpredictable, times. Writing about the Escort *Desiree* – the subject of her ethnographic study of British sex workers – O'Connell Davidson notes:

> ... days when only one or two men turn up ... A great deal of her time is spent sitting or pacing around in a state of restless boredom. She can chat to the receptionist, drink cups of coffee, endlessly reapply her make-up, but she must keep herself psychically prepared for work and cannot settle to anything else, as a punter might knock on the door at any moment (O'Connell Davidson, 1995, p.3).

Sanders (2004b) also explores the passing of time in sex work. In particular, she identifies the important role of humour and describes the way in which women sex workers spend their downtime chatting, gossiping, exchanging information and advising others.

Whilst temporality is often best understood as socially constructed, within the world of paying for sex, time is very much an objective category in which 'clock time' serves to structure and control the sexual encounter. 'Calling time' and 'going over time' are also common features of paid-for sex and indicative of the temporal institutional organisation of the sex industry. Time is a commodity but it also a symbolic entity in that time is gendered and integral to power relations. Next, we consider the temporal organisation of sex work by exploring men's experiences of time and the relationship between this and identity.

The Commodification of Time and Pleasure

Whilst it can be argued that women's bodies and emotions are commodified, most commonly, sex is sold in segments of time; for example, half an hour, an hour or overnight:

> WOW! what a treat I was in for, Her welcoming smile told me straight away, that I was in for a session to remember ... I soon wished I had booked her for two hours, well with only an hour to play I soon asked her where the bed room was ... [Ace of Diamonds, #4]

> As I had an hour booked there was time to try most things – covered BJ, sex with Sarah on top, doggie and then missionary and then finally watch as Sarah used her vibrator on herself. [Macman, #142]

> Will I be back, I have already booked her for an overnight. Watch it though, this can be addictive. [Slappy, #226]

Time is also a social experience in that sex workers are expected to give men a 'good time', for example:

> All in all this was two hours of intimate bliss. A great girl who worked hard to give me a good time. [Adrian, #5]

> ... she makes sure you have a good time. Jacqui is definitely a good find and I will be back for sure. [Eddie, #67]

Time is a symbolic marker in that power equals the control of time and those who wait are usually those who are powerless. For example, Freund and Maguire argue:

> Control over time – our own or other people's – is a form of power. Powerful persons have the ability to regulate other people's time and labour. The ability to manage our own schedules is limited by our position in society ... Time is socially organised, and the ability to schedule time and to manage it is socially distributed. Those with more power have more control over time (Freund and Maguire, 1999, pp.89-90).

Thus, time is often also gendered in that men often have more power than women and it is women who usually wait for, or on, men. The commodification of time is therefore understood differently, according to status and social group, in that some people's time is considered more valuable than that of others. The convenience of paying for sex is attractive in that men need not waste their own time. The data highlights the fact men dislike hanging around and prefer a quick and efficient service:

> i was offered a drink by the maid although I did not have to wait long. [Macman, #142]

> A minor quibble is that although an appointment system is in operation I often seem to end up waiting 15-25 mins even though I've turned up on time. [Tommo, #230]

PunterNet also warns men of the way in which their time may be manipulated by those within the sex industry. For example, in their 'Beginners Guide to Saunas and Massage Parlours', they caution:

> if the girl is busy and then you may decide to wait for her to come free. It's then a case of sitting in the lounge until she's ready. Be aware that the receptionist will always say the girl will be free earlier than she really will be, just to keep you there in case you don't fancy a long wait. Be aware in some places ... the number of girls exceeds the number of rooms and you may have to wait for a room to be come free.

Turning Tricks and Time Management

Previous research indicates that time management, or turning tricks, is an important part of the way that sex workers manage commercial sex. Our analysis of the data reveals considerable detailing of dissatisfaction with sexual encounters during which men felt rushed and in some circumstances, when men were not able to achieve ejaculation. *Kinkybeast* and *ShyBoy* state:

> The french was covered and all too brief. She started rushing me to come as soon as I started thrusting (mish). I suggested we try doggie only to be told that would cost an extra £10. I paid and she stuck a great arse at me. Again she was rushing me as soon as got started. She told me my time was up and I hadn't even come. Very disappointing. [Kinkybeast, #130]

> I started off gently but after a while she asked me to fuck harder which she enjoyed. Then disaster struck the phone rang. She informed me that we only had two minutes and suggested she finish me off by hand ... Danni seemed really disappointed and kept on apologising saying how bad she felt because it was my first time. She reassured me that if it was up to her she would have went on for longer and she told me to book longer next time so she could 'Do me good'. [ShyBoy, #222]

More confident and experienced punters such as *Flump* and *Breastcrazy* are aware that commercial sex is carefully time managed and that sex workers will call time:

> I unstripped her as far as her stockings and suspenders and started kissing her Nipples while feeling her pussy. I asked her if I could use one of her toys on her. She said yes and chose a large vibrator. I spent 5 mins or so exploring her with tongue, vibro and fingers in various positions. We then got in the 69 position and her oral technique was superb and I came after a couple of minutes. I got of the bed and she informed me I had ten minutes left so I went down on her again and finished with a fuck in missionary position. I usually use street girls ... but after this experience, I will be giving that up. [Flump, #75]

> You will be rushed by the maid who will call out after about 10 mins. I paid for a blowjob with sex. She was good but it was rushed. Wished I opted for £25 service ... Not bad for the price. [Breastcrazy, #35]

Less experienced punters, such as *Johnny W* can be disappointed when time is called, either by the sex worker or their maid:

> I asked for cum twice which was fine 'if there was enough time' … In the end it was more of a hand job, but satisfying nevertheless. At this point the door buzzer went, presumably another punter, and it was soon clear from the glances at her watch that my time was up. I left slightly disappointed. Cindy was very pleasant, but not really what I was looking for, and proceedings were slightly rushed. [Johnny W, #119]

It is commonly accepted that many sex workers will rush men and use various techniques to 'finish them off' more quickly. For a punter to be the one to rush is unusual as *Ronald* writes:

> Due to a mistake on my part I had left myself very little spare time before a business meeting and this must have been one of the few situations in which a punter had to try and hurry things up. [Ronald, #206]

Squeezing the testicles and giving hand relief during oral sex are some of the techniques used to bring men to ejaculation and, hence, usually bringing the encounter to a close. This was noted, for example, by O'Connell Davidson (1995) in her ethnographic study of British sex worker, *Desiree*. *Desiree* explains how she practises a five-stage routine with all clients which involves 'settling him in', 'getting him going', 'getting him to shoot his load', 'reassuring him' and, 'normalizing him and getting him out'. She also ensures a rapid turnaround by exercising her pelvic floor muscles to 'milk' a man, therefore getting him to come more quickly. Sanders (2005) study also confirms this in that she describes how women used timing as a technique to minimize the amount of time working and the maximum about of money earned. Men – wary of such techniques – tend to review the sex workers who use them unfavourably. Aware of this, one punter, states:

> … started with doggy, very enjoyable trust me, she was not grapping at my balls, like some girls trying to make me come quick. [Bigfoot, #24]

What seems important for punters is feeling sure that they have not been 'ripped off' or 'tricked'. As we have argued in earlier chapters, whilst aware of the 'con', individuals do not like to think of themselves as those who 'can be taken in by anything' (Goffman, 1952, p.452). The term 'trick', a synonym sometimes used to describe men who pay for sex (Holzman and Pine, 1982), is derived from the belief that sex workers trick a man 'by taking money for doing what women should do for free' (Milner and Milner, 1972, p.38).

So, whilst temporal routine and sexual practises thus serve to frame the sexual encounter, unlike outdoor sex work which is usually a more speedy and efficient transaction, indoor work requires the careful management of time.

Tick-tock: Women Who Clock Watch

Men's accounts make a clear distinction between sex workers who 'clock-watch' and those who do not or, at least, those who do not appear to do so. Given the importance of maximising income, clock watching is an important feature of indoor sex work. Ecstavasia, noting the advice given by an escort, makes the following point:

> So you get in the elevator and you go on up. Before you knock on the client's door, be sure to check your watch, because it's important to know what time you arrived – and nobody likes a clock-watcher. Incidentally, it's helpful to wear a watch that's easy to read in a dim light with just a glance (Ecstavasia, 1994, pp.187-8).

As she rightly notes, nobody likes a clock-watcher:

> ... she was clock watching and called time immediately the hour was up. [Da69er, #51]

Many of the more satisfied punters expressed their satisfaction in terms of the lack of clock-watching, for example:

> The time seems to fly by but there is no clock watching. [Visitor, #237]

> She really enjoys her work and is not a clock watcher. I would reccomend her to anyone. [Big K, #22]

> This was a really fine experience, and not in the same league as the run-of-the-mill session with a bored and silent clock-watcher. [Lancealot, #132]

Paying for sex is a leisure activity and, understandably, men wish to emerge from a commercial sexual encounter with their identities intact – if not bolstered. Obvious clock-watching reminds men that they are *paying* for sex. Men clearly recognize the existence of women's time-management. However, some punters described experiences in which they believed that time ran away for women. For example, *Baron* states:

> I went back down for some more oral while my cock recovered and thats when she forgot the clock altogether. i like to eat pussy, and she had no intention of hurrying me up. [Baron, #16]

A few of the field reports indicate that sex workers sometimes give punters extra time. This is good VFM, as *Nobbin the Nob*, points out:

> ... she did not rush me at any time, although I didn't hang around either. In all, the encounter was probably more like 15 minutes than the agreed 10, so I figured I did well considering. [Nobbin the Nob, #170]

It highlights the way that sex workers control time and are able to manipulate time in order to flatter their punters – for example:

Although we were well over the hour by now, by about 15 minutes, Jasmine stayed where she was, for another 10 minutes chatting very articulately and intelligently, all the while gently stroking and touching both by me and her. [Anon Chris, #10]

The meal took longer than i had thought and it was 9:00 pm by the time we got to her flat in Gateshead. I thought i would have to rush the sex and spoil the night but Angie said there was no rush and gave me an extra 30 mins which was great. [Legman, #134]

At the beginning of this chapter, we posed the following question: who is in control – sex workers – or the men who pay for sex? We firmly believe that power is not a monolithic category, but one that is enacted through interaction. Commercial sex, especially indoor work, is a delicate interaction between men and women. Whilst it is not possible to conclude that the sex worker is in control, it must be recognized that she does control her time and possesses the skills and techniques that enable her to do so. Men's concerns with women who rush or clock-watch can be perceived in one of two ways, both of which indicate their lack of control over the situation and their attempts to resist this. First, it can be seen simply as an attempt to manipulate the encounter and get VFM, particularly by ensuring that they achieve ejaculation. Second, the sex worker who rushes or clock-watches is clearly indicating either her lack of interest or, at least, the fact that she has something better to do (even if that is seeing another punter). This is yet another reminder to men that this is not a consensual non-commercial encounter but one for which they are a paying customer only.

Time, Power and Value-for-money

Analysis of the accounts presented here indicate that VFM is defined in terms of the sale of time or sex act and judged largely within the context of women's physical objectification and commodification of emotion. As *Nomddepc* neatly summarizes in one of his field reports:

Lady = attractive and sexy
Lady's Emotional Input = Good
Service = excellent
Value for Money = Good
Recommended: Yes
Would You Return: Yes [Nomddepc, #171]

It seems, then, that sex workers need to 'give', or at least appear to give, a great deal if they are to be perceived as successful. However, simply because sex workers give something of themselves, does not necessarily imply that that are being reduced to passive objects. It could be argued that they are powerful actors making a living within a pre-existing and socially constructed sexual order (Chapkis, 1997). In the context of paying for sex, we might argue that it is the punter's identity which is the most threatened and, subsequently, that is the sex worker who wields the greatest power. The field reports suggest that a concern with VFM is often seen as reductionist and the punter's desire for responsive, engaging women with whom they can talk also signifies a desire to disassociate with the sleaze, or stigma, of being someone who needs to, or chooses to, pay for sex.

It is fair to say that men's accounts of paying for sex dedicate considerable attention to the management of time. As Fox (1999) argues, time is a tool of power and control as well as one of resistance and, usually, the social group with the greatest power is that which wields control over time. However, the field reports indicate that sex workers are firmly in control of time and that it is the punter who seeks to resist control. The sex worker calls time, or may give extra time. The punter resists the sex worker's control through his reproach of anyone who seeks to rush him or of anyone who is obviously watching the clock. He may simply be wishing to maximize his VFM; that is, if he pays a sex worker £50 for ½ hour then he will expect to spend ½ an hour in her company. However, clock-watching also serves to remind him that he is paying for sex rather than engaging in a consensual non-commercial relationship, further threatening his sense of self.

The various ways in which sex workers can be exploited are discussed at length elsewhere (see for example, Raymond, 1998). However, the purpose of this chapter has been to explore how sex workers exercise agency in relation to the control of time and money with the commercial sexual encounter. In summary, whilst sex workers are often depicted as helpless victims, empirical studies of women sex workers portray images of both power *and* powerlessness, of choice *and* control, as well as exclusion *and* exploitation (Sharp and Earle, 2003). Whilst we are not arguing that men are 'victims', we do argue that paying for sex threatens men's self-identity, especially the maintenance of an hegemonic heterosexual masculinity. The data suggest that within the context of paying-for-sex, it is the sex worker who is in control, using clock time as a tool to empower herself when she sells sex to men.

Chapter 7

Health, Risk and Sex Work

Unpacking Some Epistemological Tensions

Of what relevance is this book in the real world of sex work? This question is not unique to our research but is one that has concerned all sociologists, and social scientists, at one time or another. Sociological knowledge cannot easily be applied if its validity is in question and, whilst the question of validity applies equally to all forms of sociological knowledge, the use of our particular methodological approach raises distinct questions concerning the validity of our research findings and the extent to which this research can be applied to the real world of sex work. Although practical application in the 'real world' has not been the primary focus of our endeavour the application of sociological knowledge should be, arguably, of concern to all those who engage in sociological thinking and research.

In this chapter, we draw together some of the threads of our research by refocusing on some of the key epistemological tensions raised in Chapter 2. Here we think about the extent to which our work can be used to understand and inform contemporary public health within the remits of contemporary public health and healthy sex promotion. In particular, we concern ourselves with whether our research is of value within the real world and focus on the extent to which men's cyber accounts of commercial sex can be accepted *prima facie* as *bona-fide* accounts of real events, or not. To accomplish this we consider the relationships between health, risk and sex work.

Health, Risk and Sex Work

Sex and the Public Health

The ever rising numbers of people infected with HIV and the increase in other sexually transmitted infections have placed healthy sex promotion high on the agenda for policy makers and others. Good sexual health is widely acknowledged as an important factor in the maintenance of overall health. It is argued that positive sexual health is beneficial for all, both in relation to physical health and psycho-social well-being:

> Sexual health is an important part of physical and mental health. It is a key part of our identity as human beings together with the fundamental human rights to privacy, a family life and living free from discrimination. Essential elements of good sexual health are

equitable relationships and sexual fulfilment with access to information and services to avoid the risk of unintended pregnancy, illness or disease (DoH, 2001, p.5).

Poor sexual health is considered to be an increasing public health problem, causing both premature death and preventable morbidity (DoH, 2001). Sexual ill health can affect all age groups and sections of society but it is not equally distributed. It especially harms vulnerable groups such as young people, minority ethnic groups and those experiencing poverty and social exclusion (for example, see Lacey *et al.*, 1997 and Hughes *et al.*, 2000). The prevention of sexual ill health is important for individuals but would also greatly reduce the significant burden on providers of health and social care (Kinghorn, 2001).

In the UK, chlamydia is now the most common diagnosis in GUM clinics. Figures show that 89,431 new diagnoses were reported in 2003, representing a 66 per cent increase in chlamydia since 1999 (The UK Collaborative Group for HIV and STI Surveillance, 2004). Studies of epidemiological data also show that gonorrhoea, which is the second most commonly diagnosed sexually transmitted bacterial infection in the UK, has more than doubled in the last ten years. Diagnostic rates of gonococcal infection have also increased in all age groups since 1995, with the highest rates seen among men aged from 20 to 24 years and women aged from 16 to 19 years (HPA, 2004). HIV infection is also increasing and it is now estimated that there are 53,000 people living with HIV in the UK; this compares to 49,500 in 2002. Whilst men who have sex with men are still the group most at risk for acquiring HIV in the UK, in 2003 58 per cent of newly diagnosed cases of HIV were in heterosexual men and women (The UK Collaborative Group for HIV and STI Surveillance, 2004). Rates of syphilitic infection, which had remained stable during the 1990s, also doubled between 1998 and 2000 (Doherty *et al.*, 2002) and the incidence of genital herpes, is thought to be on the increase too (Drake *et al.*, 2000).

Holland, Ramazanoglu and Scott have argued that the 'AIDS epidemic has brought together sex, deviance and death in ways which have provoked both widespread fear of infection and also horror of the infected' (1990, p.499). Sex workers, whilst they may indeed be healthy, are widely regarded as members of the so-called high-risk groups for sexually transmitted infections and HIV. As Wojcicki and Malala (2001) suggest, if they lack access to economic resources, they may have to choose between economic survival and possible exposure to sexually transmitted infection; violence and rape may further expose such women to HIV infection. Sex workers are also one of the groups seen as responsible – whether deliberately or through their otherwise dangerous behaviours – for the epidemic of HIV and for its continuing spread. Wilton argues: 'Particularly notable is the insistence of many AIDS researchers on regarding sex work as a *sexual* rather than a *commercial* encounter – and consequently sex workers themselves as sexually promiscuous individuals, rather than a segment of the labour force enduring appalling working conditions' (1999, p.189). Within the context of this epidemic, Holland, Ramazanoglu and Scott also argue that:

moral majorities have exploited the opportunity to promote reactions against ... any sexuality outside monogamous, heterosexual marriage ... This mode of thinking makes prostitutes, rather than their clients, responsible for safe sex, and it is prostitutes rather than their clients who are the focus of control ... Policies are aimed at protecting the client from the infected prostitute (Holland, Ramazanoglu and Scott, 1990, p.508).

So whilst 'women' – as in white, heterosexual and middle-class, 'everybody's sister, wife and mother' type of woman (Kitzinger, 1994, p.95) - remain invisible in mainstream discourses of HIV and AIDS, female sex workers have been centre stage in representations of sexuality and disease. Both historically, and in contemporary accounts, sex work has been construed within the framework of sexual health. This, Tiefer (1995) argues, serves to place sex work within a medical framework emphasising an assumption of deviance, universality, individualism and biological reductionism. This, she continues, places sex within an unhelpful paradigm. Also, as Butcher (1994) notes, public attention has fallen on the sex worker, as though she were acting on her own, with little reference made to the punters, pimps, maids or managers within which health, risk and sex work must be understood. Indeed there has long been a strong, perceived association between prostitution and disease. As we have already discussed in Chapter 1, sex workers are seen as wilfully engaged in both criminal conduct and the spread of contagion and, over time, have been subject to intense official scrutiny and criminal sanctions (Scott, 2003). Indeed, sex workers have been held responsible for everything 'from the fall of empires to the spread of venereal disease' (Wilton, 1999, p.189).

Across the countries of the UK, as within other countries and cultures (see Palmer, 2004) talking about sex is often taboo and individuals can have limited vocabularies for talking about sexual behaviour (Spencer, Faulkner and Keegan, 1988). Studies of young people show that they are often embarrassed to talk about sexual health and that they are concerned with issues of confidentiality and disclosure (Petchey, Farnsworth and Heron 2001; Churchill *et al.*, 2000). Health workers, too, can often find it difficult to talk about sex candidly. For example, Tomlinson argues that, 'Many doctors are concerned about their ability to take an appropriate history from a patient with a sexual problem' (1998, p.1573) and some research suggests that this may be the case because health professionals are too embarrassed to talk about sex (Earle and Evans, 2004). Concerns have also been expressed over lack of clinical knowledge and expertise amongst health professionals in dealing with HIV and other sexually transmitted infections (DoH, 2001).

Previous research on HIV and AIDS has shown how little we know about sexual practices and has identified a need to deconstruct our knowledge in order to make sense of people's experiences (Holland, Ramazanoglu and Scott, 1990). In this chapter we explore men's accounts of their sexual behaviour within the specific context of risk and 'un/safe' sexual practices.

Risk, Health and Sex Work

In Beck's (1992, p.114) influential work on the 'risk society', he argues that heterosex has changed considerably in that 'intimacies can be exchanged ... almost like handshakes ...'. Drawing on Beck's work, Skidmore and Hayter (2000) suggest that risk has changed the nature of society and that the rules by which individuals engage with society are now negotiated on personal, rather than group, levels. Whilst this may be generally the case, Beck's concept of risk society has been widely criticized (see, for example, Adkins 2002). In *PunterNet.com* we see examples of the way in which men manage and construct personal narratives of risk and sex work as well as evidence of commonly held norms which are created, maintained and reinforced at group level.

Understanding 'risk' is important if we are to explore men's cyber-accounts in relation to 'un/safe' sex within the commercial encounter. Contemporary discourses of sexual behaviour are mediated within the context of risk and, in relation to the public health agenda, mediated and managed within the context of surveillance medicine. Armstrong's (1995) work positions surveillance medicine within the context of a self-reflexive responsibilized subject in which responsibility for surveillance is given to individuals themselves. He argues:

> Concerns with diet, exercise, stress, sex, etc. become the vehicles for encouraging the community to survey itself. The ultimate triumph of Surveillance Medicine would be its internalization by all the population (Armstrong, 1995, pp.399-400).

There is a considerable volume of already published material in the field of risk and risk-taking. Most research has assumed that risk behaviour is based on individualist and rationalistic assumptions. The health belief model (Becker, 1984) for example – which has suffered from extensive criticism – assumes that once individuals are advised on the appropriate actions, they will voluntarily and willingly refrain from risky practices. Similar theories and models such as the theory of reasoned action and planned behaviour (Ajzen and Fishbein, 1980) have been similarly criticized.

Social constructionist approaches, on the other hand, recognize the individual within the context in which she or he operates. Whittaker and Hart's (1996) study of sex work, for example, attempted to show how women's behaviours were constrained by financial pressures and other demands. From this analysis they have argued:

> Rather than focus on women's self-efficacy or health beliefs ... it is through the social organisation of their work that we are best able to understand the nature of their risk exposure, and their strategies for managing risk in relation to their occupational health (Whittaker and Hart, 1996, p.399)

Our discussion of health, risk and sex work seeks to locate men's behaviour within a framework that includes both an appreciation both rational agency and the constraints posed by place and space and power relations.

'Safe' Sex

Neighbourhood and Location

Within the context of STI prevention, the concept of 'safe' sex usually refers to the safety of sexual practices and, to some extent, the prevention of pregnancy. Many writers have also explored safe sex within the context of power and agency (for example, Holland et al., 1998).

Men's cyber accounts make specific reference to whether experiences were considered to be safe or not. However, within this context, 'safety' takes on a number of distinct meanings. In men's cyber-accounts, safety can refer to the location and visibility of the venue and surrounding neighbourhood. Ryan (1994) argues that spaces and places become defined in relation to structured and prevailing relations of power. Areas designated as 'red-light' districts, for example, come to be defined over time and through negotiations played out between sex workers, pimps, punters, residents and the police. O'Neill (2001) argues that the power relations of spaces and places must also be defined in terms of gender, class and race, suggesting that clearly defined areas of prostitution are, typically, located in poorer, multi-racial neighbourhoods. Most of the accounts on *PunterNet* indicate that punters specifically seek out locations that are the exact opposite of this. 'Dodgy' areas, as men sometimes describe them, are undesirable, whereas the most desirable location would be a nice suburban neighbourhood, with good street lighting and good security. The following extract provides a good example of this commonly expressed view, emphasising the importance of the 'respectable' neighbourhood:

> A clean, cosy, peaceful and comfortable ground floor flat offering the major amenities in a pleasantly quiet and respectable centrally located neighbourhood. I have never felt other than safe, for although there are other flats in the house, the residents are rarely heard and even more rarely seen. There is plenty of adequately safe and discreet on-street parking adjacent and nearby. [Antonym, #11]

As indicated by *Antonym*'s extract, punters also frequently made explicit references about the safety of their cars, for example:

> Area not too bad parking no problem and feels safe enough. [Pokey, #187]

> Kareens is quite a long established flat in the Southside of Edinburgh, next to the Royal College of Surgeons and opposite the Festival Theatre. It is a safe enough area, as long as you don't have too flashy a car. [Wavygravy, #227]

Visibility of the location was also important. For some men, venues that were obviously not in 'red light' areas were more desirable. Walk-ups located in busy high streets were considered risky, particularly during the day. Discrete locations are highly prized as it makes it less likely that a punter will be spotted entering premises known to be used by sex workers. As we have argued in Chapter 2, whilst we believe that *PunterNet* constitutes a distinct normative world, that is not to say that the men who contribute reviews are in any sense unaware of, or uninfluenced by, the wider normative world which they inhabit. The fact that they are concerned about being seen entering the premises of a sex worker demonstrates a concern with being exposed as punters and demonstrates their overall commitment to mainstream values. As the extract from *Antonym's* account indicates, suburban neighbourhoods sometimes created the problem of 'nosy neighbours' as *Billog* further describes below:

> Nice Quiet Area. House is opposite a field so no nosy neighbours across the way. [Billog, #28]

So, industrial sites were considered to be safe locations too:

> [an] 'industrial' type building set in large car park V safe. [W.H.Oami, #252]

Women working as escorts were also asked to arrive 'discretely' at the venue of choice, usually the punter's home or hotel room. This usually referred to the wearing of discrete clothing that did not obviously indicate she was a sex worker. *WildWilly2*, for example, describes the way in which Joanne arrives at his home:

> I asked [her] to arrive very discretely, which she did with a smart business suit and briefcase. She arrived on time and we sat and had a cup of tea and a chat! As mentioned previously I had asked Joanne to arrive discretely – she went upstairs to change in to a tiny, tight red dress which showed her perfect curves off along with high heeled shoes ... [WildWilly2, #246]

Been Around describes a similar experience at his hotel room, which he had booked specifically for this purpose:

> She arrived wearing a discrete business suit and carrying a briefcase. I had given her my room number and she came straight up. [Been Around, #1]

In both cases 'business suits' and 'briefcases' form the props which serve to differentiate between sex workers and 'other' women. Once, again, this serves to show the significance of avoiding exposure as a man who pays for sex and an awareness of the mainstream values and beliefs of the outside world in which paying for sex is potentially discrediting.

Some accounts also express a concern with being 'ripped off'. In one case, *Pudge* compares what he describes as a 'safe' experience, with another during which he was robbed and threatened with violence:

> I'd been here before when it was called Gabrelles. So i knew it was going to be clean, which it was. It was comfortable, clean and above all i felt safe. you guys know what i mean!!! I'd just had a very bad, unsafe experience with a girl out of the Coventry 'why' magazine – i was ripped for 20 notes, she advertises as a 19 yr old £40, 19 maybe, but lads it barked, so it cost 20 to get out or i'll call some to get you. so bye bye off i went, to find some SAFTEY in PARADISE. [Pudge, #190]

Most accounts of this nature do not, in fact, depict violence but the data suggest that punters are vulnerable to robbery and theft:

> I've only posted this report as a warning and also as a bit of entertainment for others to laugh at my expense. I was told on the phone that £70.00 covered 2 girls, everything in, and "my friend will do Anal" Went in, paid the £70.00 and the blonde knelt down unbuckled my pants and started sucking me... then i saw her hands in my trouser pockets while they were on the floor! ! recovered my credit cards, car keys and cash and stupidly stayed! ! [Preston Pete, #189]

As we have already described in previous chapters, research into sex work often focuses on the violence and abuse perpetrated by (male) clients against (female) sex workers. In fact, female sex workers operate numerous strategies to avoid or minimize the risks of robbery and physical violence whilst working. For example, some sex workers will frequently make use of a chaperone, such as a maid or friend, to manage the risk of violence. Others will make reference to their 'boyfriends' and those who escort may be accompanied by a 'driver'. To prevent robbery, some workers will consistently take payment upfront and then hide the money whilst getting on with the transaction. Sex workers have also been known to use weapons as a method of remedial protection against violence; the use of kitchen utensils, baseball bats, lighters and bleach have been reported by sex workers as a means of preventing personal injury to themselves (Benson, 1998; McKeganey and Barnard, 1996). In Sanders' (2004a) study of indoor sex work in England, one worker, *Astrid*, states: 'We have CS gas here and everything and I wouldn't be afraid to use it. We have an alert buzzer in the bedroom and we have a pickaxe handle. And if I had my way I would kill someone if I had the chance'. Sanders' (2005) research also highlights the importance of screening within indoor work and the use of 'instinct' in deciding whether to accept or reject a client. When contacted by telephone, sex workers can screen any potential clients, and this can be interpreted as vagueness by clients:

> As others have said Diane sounds a little vague on the telephone. [Bowmore, #35]

Some of the men in our study seemed aware of this screening process, for example, writing about sex worker *Barbie-Girl*, one punter noted:

> Easily contactable by phone, and after a few calls either way so she can weed out time wasters, all was arranged. [David Murphy, #55]

Also:

> When you book for the first time, don't be surprised if you are questioned at length about yourself; Peaches is very fussy about whom she sees - if you piss her off on the phone or question her security arrangements she won't see you, but that is your loss! [Valentine, #240]

Our data, however, also suggest that not all men are aware of the strategies sex workers adopt to protect themselves from punters. For example, *booker*, describes an incident where he had arranged to meet someone on the phone who subsequently failed to show:

> Having read previous FR I contacted Sassy and arranged for her to visit me in Watford (i would pay her travelling expenses) She phoned me to confirm she was on the train and asked if I could pick up some supplies from the chemist! ! as she had not had time, which I agreed to and rung her back to confirm. Without going into the boring details she did not show, and did not call to apologise, despite repeatedly ringing her she avoided my calls and I only got voice mail, I can be a little sneaky and rung her from a call box, she was obviously in a pub but made an exscuse about her child being ill. I was very disappointed and wasted £100 on a hotel and more on a restuarant. [booker, #33]

Sanders (2005) suggests that some sex workers first come into contact with men via the telephone and that they rely on these short conversations to establish whether he is trustworthy. For example, in Sanders' study, *Anita*, who works premises, says 'You can normally tell by the manner of their voice on the phone what they are like. When you have been in the business a long time you pick up on a lot of things'. So, what could be taken as rudeness and unreliability by the punter may, in fact, just be an example of this screening process in action.

Whilst violence against women is by all accounts widespread (particularly in outdoor work), in this case we see some evidence of the exposure and vulnerability for male clients during experiences of commercial sex. Punters are concerned with safety, defined in terms of neighbourhood and discretion, as well as vulnerability to theft, robbery and physical violence. However, in our research we found no accounts of men describing actual violence or abuse, either by sex workers, maids, pimps or boyfriends.

Cleanliness, Safety and Hygiene

Notions of cleanliness and contamination are also useful in understanding men's cyber-accounts of risk and safety. However, whilst men position themselves as 'clean' and 'safe' – sex workers, their behaviours and environments – are most likely to be identified as a potential source of danger and disease. As Adkins has argued 'contaminating Others' are 'understood to be particular categories of person, for example, the "gay man", the "bisexual man" and the "female prostitute"' (2002, p.119). In this sense, punters are positioned as at risk, rather than risky, and threatened, rather than threatening. Many references are made to women and locations being 'clean'. One can infer from this that cleanliness also implies less risk and a 'safer' experience. For example:

> Her home is really very clean and tidy and having been met at the door I was shown into the living room. I never at any time felt nervous and did in fact feel very safe. [Fireblade, #73]

Room was clean and shower had soaps and shower gels, towels etc, very safe. [Dv, #66]

Reasonably clean inside, although bedsheets were slightly damp with baby oil. [Gadgeteer, #79]

The term 'being clean' is often commonly used to describe those who are free from drugs. However, of all the data analysed for this study, reference was only made to drug use on two occasions. For example, in one account, *Preston Pete* describes his experience when arriving at a parlour:

Small anorexic looking drugged up blonde no tits at all and a skinny tall drugged up brunette both hideous and spaced out. [Preston Pete, #189]

The relationship between sex, risk, drugs and hygiene have been highlighted elsewhere. For example, in McKeganey and Barnard's (1996) study of sex work in Glasgow, men made explicit references to the dangers posed by women whom they perceived to be drug users. For example, one man in their study says: 'I wouldn't have thought that any of the ones I've been with are drug users. I think if you look at some people you can tell. I mean I suppose they have injection marks on their arms and what have you, I think they also tend to be the dirtier scruffier types. I would rather pay more and go with someone who I thought was a bit cleaner. Like the girl I go with now, I know for a fact that she showers between, like, seeing me and someone else' (p.55).
    The literature also highlights the way in which women's bodies are often seen as unpredictable and uncivilized whereas the bodies of men are not (see, for example, Britton, 1998 and Martin, 1989). The unpredictable nature of women's bodies and their tendencies to leak are well documented in the literature. However, research findings show that within the context of heterosex, for men, most parts of women's bodies are within bounds, as long as they are seen to be 'clean' (Thorogood, 2000). A study of sexual behaviour amongst young people in England (Skidmore and Hayter, 2000) showed that 'describers' – the words used to describe partners with regard to lack of risk during sexual activity – often implied safety, cleanliness and previous safe sexual practice. The cleanliness of women's bodies, in particular, featured strongly in men's accounts on *PunterNet*. For example, *Zac* states:

Bailey opened the door. I was very impressed with her good looks and cleanliness and I knew I was in for a good time. [Zac, #239]

Some accounts also indicate the importance of men's own cleanliness and highlight some of the ways in which female sex workers ensure that men are clean. In one account, washing and hygiene are clearly included as part of sexual foreplay. For example:

Once you arrive you will almost certainly be taken to the bathroom and washed or given a bath – Peaches is extremely hygiene conscious – but don't worry because this is not really too bad an experience! Then you'll probably be kissed but your breath must be fresh. [Valentine, #240]

In other cases, men's accounts highlight the use of humour:

YES, she likes you to have a shower first (and YES there is a jokey sign about the wet towels), but she is always freshly showered. [Dave Brown, #53]

This reinforces the findings of research within other contexts, which suggests that humour is often used to ease potentially difficult or embarrassing situations (for example, for a discussion of humour in healthcare contexts see Billig, 2001 and Chapple and Ziebland, 2004). The use of humour in sex work has been briefly mentioned elsewhere in the literature (see Downe, 1999). Sanders' work (2004b), however, extends the discussion of humour more fully. She argues, for example that humour is used to ridicule clients, and that it is also used as a strategy to resist harassment and verbal aggression. However, we can extend this further. In our case, humour is used as a tool to reinforce and control women's expected norms concerning punters' cleanliness and hygiene.

'Safe' Sexual Practices

In our research, we were also keen to explore the more common concept of safe sex in terms of 'safe', and 'unsafe', sexual practices. One of the biggest concerns facing public health policy and practice is the question of whether sex workers use condoms and whether or not clients demand, or refuse, condom use. Previous research indicates that women sex workers are often powerless to insist on condom use by their clients (for example, see Patton, 1994 and Pyett and Warr, 1996). However, research on this subject lacks homogeneity. Other accounts indicate that sex workers can be seen as 'self-determining service providers' (Weatherall and Priestley, 2001) who are able to make choices and set and enforce rules upon their male clients. For example, *Rose*, a sex worker quoted in a study by Weatherall and Priestley (2001, p.336) in New Zealand states 'and he wanted extras and I said no I don't do them and that was really empowering to just every now and then say fuck you'.

Within our research some cyber-accounts do not explicitly mention whether or not a condom was used. For example:

By now I am ready to start giving her my hot wet cock bend her over and ram it up her tight Bum! Wow she is like a bucking bronco screaming for me to give her it harder whoops I cum wen so would you up her bum. Sandy then gives me a relaxing massage soon I am getting hard again ... now I'm ready to have that wet pussy and is she wet her legs hook around my neck and do I ram her hard ... [BigJohnUK, #25]

However, accounts such as these are unusual. It is by far more common for men's accounts to make explicit references to condom use and to express their likes and dislikes concerning the use of condoms. In only four accounts could we find a reference to the use of a condom throughout the *entire* sexual experience. For example:

> She wanted the condom on straight away and started with a body to body massage. [Meadow man, #150]

This does appear to be unusual, but when it does occur it appears to be at the woman's insistence, rather than the man's. Previous research on sex work would suggest that sex workers might lack the 'negotiating power' (Holland et al., 1998) required to insist on condom use, and that this can be explained with reference to the unequal distribution of power between men and women. Whilst this may be the case for some sex workers (and particularly for women working outdoors) there was no evidence of this within men's own accounts. The following extract is another example of condom use during the whole sexual experience, and this account is unusual as it is the only one to make explicit reference to issues of risk and sexually transmitted infections:

> Leonne was quite friendly. All services with condom – she won't do OWO because of the risk of STDs and wanted to know why I was prepared to take the risk. [Nobbin the Nob, #170]

In the third instance we found of condoms being used throughout the whole sexual experience, *Paul* sees this as evidence that she is 'clean':

> every thing is with a condom so i no she is a clean girl and im passing that information to all you people who are looking for this type of lady cos ill definatly be returning and i sujest you try it too. [#177]

We found only one example of a woman prepared only to masturbate men with a condom. *Sing* states:

> Condom on for everything – even hand relief, offered reverse oral (wouldn't want to thanks!) [#224]

However, with this single exception, the accounts claimed that masturbation was performed without a condom and they describe different techniques used by women to manage men's ejaculate. Some women allow men to ejaculate over parts of their body, such as the breasts, whereas others expect men to ejaculate into tissues:

> After a long slow session of fucking and sucking those tits, I told her that I was going to come over her tits. She removed the condom, and wanked me superbly until I shot a large load all over them. We then chatted and I left shortly after. [Lancealot, #132]

> We ended with her giving me a HJ which she got me to catch in a tissue. [Confuscius, #48]

Turning now to intercourse, it is worth noting that no direct references to penis-vagina intercourse *without* a condom were made in men's cyber accounts. In one account, *Reuters* [#199] states that his punt: 'Would do most things uncovered for a fee'. Interestingly, he makes no specific references to which sex acts took place or whether these took place with or without a condom. The *PunterNet* site recommends that men use condoms. So either we can infer that condoms are always used for penis-vagina intercourse, or that men choose not to disclose the fact that they are engaging in this type of unsafe sex, for fear of transgressing what appears to be an expected norm amongst punters (or, at least, amongst those involved in the normative world of *PunterNet.com*). This is not dissimilar to what has been reported about sex workers elsewhere. For example, Sanders (2004a) suggests that indoor sex workers vehemently conform to the expectations of condom use. And, moreover, that this is regulated within the moral hierarchy of the indoor sex market which places such expectations on women.

Previous studies have shown that male clients often discount the personal risk of sexually transmitted infections, either by arguing that they have infallible personal strategies for safety or that no such strategies for safety can be taken (see Plumridge *et al.*, 1997). However, accounts indicate that condom use is widespread and often considered mandatory as the following extracts indicate:

> I slipped on the rubber jacket and entered her very, very tight tunnel –missionary style ... [WildWilly2, #246]

> Eventually she put the obligatory condom on me and climbed aboard for some frantic 'reverse cowgirl' followed by doggie position. [Dv, #66]

With respect to anal intercourse, again no references were made to sex without the use of a condom, and condom use was an expectation. Particular references are also made to the use of thicker, extra strength condoms during anal sex, for example:

> She then got some extra strength condoms out and asked me to grease her anus with KY jelly. This took about 2-3 minutes, after which I was laid down, she got! on top facing me and she inserted my now purple member into her 'VERY' tight ass saying things like 'do you like fucking whores in the ass baby?' ... it felt like fucking heaven! [Arroganza, #12]

> PLEASE TELL ALL GIRLS THAT LOOSE FITTING CONDOMS –ON THE TIP–ARE INFINITELY MORE FUN, AND THEY DO STAY ON! Likewise, the sheet rubber ones really do delay action and ruin the job for us front door men. I do understand that inch thick ones are needed round the back. [2xanite, #2]

In an anal sex guide for women, Taormino (1998) suggests that the person being penetrated can be especially vulnerable, both physically and emotionally, especially given the intensely taboo nature of anal sex. Extending this argument, Greer (1999, p.6) states:

Penetration equals domination in the animal world and therefore in the unregenerate human world which is part of it. The penetree, regardless of sex, cannot rule, OK. Not in prison, not in the army, not in business, not in the suburbs. The person on the receiving end is fucked, finished, unserviceable, degraded.

Drawing on a Foucauldian perspective, however, Kippax and Smith (2001) suggest that power dynamics in anal intercourse need to be contextualized, arguing that the person being acted upon (the penetree) must be recognized as a person who acts, as well as a person who makes choices. Men's accounts indicate that not all sex workers offer anal sex or, at least, they do not offer it to all punters. They also indicate that anal sex is often more expensive than other sex acts: For example:

She has her rules (no anal) and does not like her nipples touched but gives a great BJ & sex. [Jode 1, #115]

She is pleasant and chatty and will do most things except anal she is new to the scene but know how to please. [John Boy, #116]

Anal was on the menu – not sure if available though. [Meadow man, #150]

will do anal (cost extra). [Minge Eater, #156]

Just because condom use for vaginal and anal intercourse is expected, this does not mean that men do not express dissatisfaction. This is implicit in the following account by *Anon Chris*:

Although it was very enjoyable and Jasmine was extremely enthusiastic, I couldn't finish, probably due to the condom, so I opted for HR to finish which was successful ... [Anon Chris, #10]

Oral sex is thought to be one of the most commonly performed services within the sex industry (McKeganey and Barnard, 1996). References to oral sex commonly appear in men's accounts on *PunterNet* and accounts show that this is performed both with and without a condom. Whilst medical knowledge is transient and uncertain, research suggests that oral sex does have the potential to transmit HIV (Gottlieb, 2003). However, this is contested. Oral sex has also been linked to the increasing number of diagnoses for syphilitic infection and has been identified as the most common route for the transmission of genital herpes (Doherty, *et al.*, 2002; Drake, *et al.*, 2000). There is evidence to suggest that sex workers believe oral sex to be far less risky than other forms of sex. For example, McKeganey and Barnard (1996, p.30) state, 'One woman said that she had stopped doing sex with clients and now only did gams [oral sex]. She said that four and a half months ago a condom had burst during full sex. As a result she felt that sex was too dangerous. She had had an HIV test in response to this and the test had been negative'.

In the following extracts we see some examples where oral sex on men is practised using a condom. For some, like *Mr T.*, *Casca* and *Confucius*, the use of condoms does not detract from their pleasure and overall satisfaction with the experience:

> with no rush and keen to try most things... all safe sex blow jobs are superb ... [Mr T, #161]

> She then put a condom on me with her mouth and did a little oral which was pretty good. [Casca, #41]

> First oral, even with a condom it was great ... [Legman, #134]

For others, the use of condoms does detract from their enjoyment, as *Flash* describes:

> She put a condom on for oral, although I asked politely for without. A five minute suck and quick poke was all I was allowed. So much for paying for half an hour, but I didn't exactly feel like staying any longer! Very disappointing, especially after reading other posts about this sauna. [Flash, #74]

However, oral sex *without* the use of a condom, sometimes described in *PunterNet* as OWO (Oral Without) or as BBBJ (Bare Back Blow Job), was very frequently described in men's accounts:

> She has the longest tongue I've ever seen, and somehow then started licking just under my balls and around my arse. Heaven! She then asked me to turn over and started licking my cock and sucking my balls uncovered. [Andy, #9]

The following accounts clearly show that condoms are not always used. One less experienced punter, who describes himself as *Shyboy*, is surprised to receive oral-without during his first paid-for experience:

> Being my first time I could hardly believe that she was doing it [oral] without a condom ... great! ! ! ! [Shyboy, #222]

Just as with masturbation, men's accounts show that women use different techniques for dealing with men's ejaculate when performing oral sex. Some women will perform oral without a condom and will allow men to ejaculate within their mouths, for example:

> I opted for a nice 69'er, which soon after commencement I came in her lovely mouth ... [Bigshagger, #26]

> when I'd reached boiling point, I asked her to finish me off orally. She did this expertly, and swallowed absolutely everything. [Daveinascot, #54]

> Then she begged me to fuck her mouth which I did so obligingly, but I couldn't hold my spunk any longer and filled her mouth, which she swallowed greedily. [Johnathon, #118]

Like anal sex, some accounts indicate that swallowing carries a financial premium:

> Rather than have her swallow it I urged her to kiss me with her sperm covered mouth. (To swallow costs £10 extra) [Prono P, #188]

Swallowing appears to be the preferred option and much discussion is had about whether particular women will or won't swallow, as the following accounts demonstrate:

> Don't know if she swallows, since I was so lost in the experience I came without pushing this – another thing for next time! [Silkcut, #223]

Other women choose to spit the ejaculate out. A clear distinction is thus made between those women that spit and those that will swallow, with the latter being men's much preferred option. For example:

> Nice OWO, a bit of reverse and then her turn again. She swallowed, but made it clear she was going to the bathroom to spit. [BJ Friend, #29]

> I heard reports that she swallows but in my case most of my cum was spat back on my dick. Is she trying to say my cum isn't good enuff??? [Billog, #28]

Other women will offer oral without a condom but prefer men not to ejaculate in their mouths; this is often described as oral without, but not to completion:

> Started to undress each other and she gave me a body-to-body massage. Started kissing before she gave me oral (without but not to completion). [Zac, #239]

> Oral sex followed without condom but not to completion. [Manitou, #144]

Very little discussion on women's management of ejaculation and ejaculate can be found in previous studies of sex work. However, a study of male sex workers in France illustrates how male *gigolos*, whilst unlikely to perform oral sex with a condom, will not allow clients to ejaculate within the mouth. This, Laurindo da Silva (1999) argues, they see as 'protecting' themselves from sexually transmitted infections. Thorogood's concept of 'mouthrules' is also useful here in that she argues how 'the "rules" which govern what we do with our mouths, for example, what we will or will not put into them, are central to the production of particular gender and sexual identities' (2000, p.179). Drawing on the work of Douglas (1966) she suggests that mouthrules can be organized along two axes; the boundaries between differing socially organized people and the hierarchical ordering of members, through rules, across groups. For the purposes of understanding commercial oral sex these axes may draw distinctions between strangers and intimate others, and sex workers and their clients, positioning the latter in a zone of ambivalence. It may also help us to understand how personal adherence to mouthrules (i.e. no completion in mouth) is mediated through both levels of personal strictness and the hierarchical ordering of sex workers and their clients. Women's reluctance, and refusal, to perform oral sex to completion signifies levels of adherence to mouthrules which are not congruent with the notions of paying for sex. One punter describes his experience:

> after telling me again it was £50 for oral without to completion, the girl came in and told me I could cum anywhere but near the face, I understand 'to completion' to mean cim but was told under no circumstances that it wasn't and it was a problem as the money was entered into the book! Anyway simply the worst experience I have had in a long long time and I personally wouldn't send my worst enemy their. She told me I could cum on her breasts and then moaned at how messy it was! The only consolation was that she dropped the dirty dripping tissues right in her lap and had to run off and wash! A fitting end to an awful experience. Avoid like the plague! [Big Guy 58, #27]

There are clear differences in practise and preference with relation to oral sex but some accounts point to the fact that men purposely seek out women who will perform oral sex, specifically to completion and without the use of a condom:

> I was interested in BBBJ till completion and only Monique offered that which was the reason I chose her. [Bob, #31]

Concluding Thoughts: Managing Risks

It is important to move away from an understanding of sex work as one in which sex workers are the victims of their male clients. Within this context, sex workers are powerless in their negotiations over safe sex and this both contributes to the continuation of their victim status and continues the stigmatisation of the sex work industry. Within the context of public health and healthy sex promotion, Wojcicki and Malala argue that, 'A public health discourse that focuses on the decisions that sex workers make in their daily lives and the *reasons* behind these *decisions* can help advance a more humane public health' (2001, p.102). Extending this, we argue that by recognising and exploring men's narratives, we may be able to understand power relations between female sex workers and their clients and better understand the relationships between health, risk and sex work.

Rhodes and Cusick (2002) argue that the issue of unprotected sex is not a morally neutral one, but one which is subject to competing interpretations of risk, acceptability and moral responsibility. Men's cyber accounts are, thus, moral enterprises whereby images of risk and responsibility are created. What, then, can we learn from men's accounts and how can we apply what we learn to the real world of sex work?

Rhodes and Cusick suggest:

> Accounts of risk management are risk managed. Like all social interactions, accounts are situated representations of particular phenomena ... Risk accounts speak as much about wider perceptions of acceptability associated with certain risk behaviours as the reasons why these behaviours occur (Rhodes and Cusick, 2002, p.212).

Men's accounts tell us that unprotected vaginal and anal intercourse are considered taboo within the *PunterNet* community. Previous research on indoor sex work indicates that this is also the case for women themselves and that women who do not consistently use condoms risk transgression of the moral hierarchy of indoor sex work. If men's accounts are to be accepted *prima facia* as recollections of real events then they would suggest that, within this context, condom use is widespread; and, indeed, that particular attention is given to condom strength within the context of anal sex. This prohibition is reinforced (and re/created) by the normative expectations of the *PunterNet* website which asserts, what it undoubtedly sees as, its moral responsibility for the prevention of sexually transmitted infections and HIV.

However, even if these accounts are essentially bogus, works of fiction, merely narrative representations of self then they still tell us an awful lot about risk and the way in which risks are managed and understood. Although specific reference to sexually transmitted infection and HIV are rarely evident within men's accounts, concerns with cleanliness, safety and hygiene are apparent. Condom use is reported as expected, widespread and routine; the need for condom use can therefore be read as implicit within men's accounts. In relation to vaginal and anal intercourse, it would, indeed, be the practise of unprotected sex, which would require considerable accounting for.

The same cannot be said, however, in the case of oral sex. Here, and in relation to the concerns of a public health agenda, there does seem to be a lack of knowledge concerning the potential reported health risks associated with oral transmission of STIs or HIV. This is not entirely surprising given the reported lack of knowledge amongst the general population as a whole, and amongst health and social care workers (for example, see Doherty *et al.*, 2002). Once again, if men's cyber accounts are accepted as recollections of real events then wide variations in preferences and practices are evident. At one extreme, some sex workers are performing oral sex with a condom and, according to men's accounts, always perform oral sex in this way. At the other extreme, others will perform oral sex without a condom, will allow men to ejaculate in their mouths and will swallow the ejaculate. Given our interest in agency, it is interesting to note that, whilst men seem to exhibit a strong preference for unprotected oral sex, rules concerning condom use are established and maintained by women, and not their clients. Furthermore, men's accounts show that women's 'mouthrules' are those which dictate when and how ejaculate is managed within this particular context.

Previous accounts of non-commercial unprotected sex suggest that various discourses of risk exist as a means of risk managing accounts of risky behaviours. For example, Rhodes and Cusick's (2002) study of HIV positive people indicate recourse to notions of powerlessness, inebriation, lack of knowledge, and biological drive, amongst others. So, even if men's sexual stories are 'bogus', within the context of 'real world' research they do tell us something about perceptions and expectations of un/protected oral sex. Men's cyber-accounts, although exhibiting some diversity, create a normative acceptance of unprotected oral sex within the *PunterNet* community.

Men's attitudes to condoms and condom use have been widely researched. Vitellone, for example, writes:

> Heterosexual men's apparent aversion to wearing condoms in AIDS culture has lead a range of analysts and researchers to ask why this is the case ... the answer to this question lies in the way the practice of unsafe heterosex – without condoms – is the key for the constitution of a hegemonic heterosexual masculine self-identity ... as a spontaneous, uninterruptible, powerful, hydraulic force ... (Vitellone, 2000, p.152).

Studies of condom (non)use indicate that men's 'aversion to latex' exists for a number of reasons. A study of young heterosexual men (Flood, 2003) shows that many men believe that condom use reduces penile sensation. The same study also indicates that condoms are thought to interrupt spontaneity and ruin 'the heat of the moment'. Flood argues:

> The 'heat of the moment' is 'hot' because it involves the literal heat of two bodies in physical contact and both participants are 'hot' in the thrall of sexual passion or lust. Condoms *kill* this moment: either condoms cannot be incorporated into the episode, or they are unwelcome intrusions which interrupt and spoil the moment ... Condoms represent the intrusion of the practical, responsible and mundane into a space that is impractical, irresponsible and ethereal (Flood, 2003, p.360).

In the context of commercial sex, and in relation to some of the ideas we have discussed in previous chapters, condom use – at least for oral sex – is an intrusion into the irresponsible and lustful nature of paying for sex. In many ways, it may also disrupt men's perceptions of female pleasure, passion and lust and, in particular, disrupt their identities as men who do, but do not need to, pay for sex.

Bibliography

Acton, W. (1972) [1870], *Prostitution Considered in its Moral, Social, and Sanitary Aspects in London and other Large Cities and Garrison Towns with Proposals for the Control and Prevention of its Attendant Evils*, Frank Cass & Co., London.

Adam, B. (1990), *Time and Social Theory*, Polity Press, Oxford.

Adkins, L. (2002), *Revisions: gender & sexuality in late modernity*, Open University Press, Buckingham.

Ajzen, I. and Fishbein, M. (1980), *Understanding Attitudes and Predicting Social Behaviour*, Prentice Hall, New Jersey.

Allen, L. (2003), 'Girls Want Sex, Boys Want Love: Resisting Dominant Discourses of (Hetero)sexuality', *Sexualities*, Vol. 6(2), pp. 1363-4607.

Armstrong, D. (1995), 'The rise of surveillance medicine', *Sociology of Health & Illness*, Vol. 17(3), pp. 393-404.

Atchison, A., Fraser, L. and Lowman, J. (1998), 'Men who buy sex: Preliminary findings of an exploratory study', in J.E. Elias, V.L. Bullough, V. Elias and G. Brewer (eds), *Prostitution: On Whores, Hustlers and Johns*, Prometheus Books, New York.

Battersby, C. (1998), *The Phenomenal Woman: Feminist Metaphysics and the Patterns of Identity*, Polity Press, Cambridge.

Bechar-Israeli, H. (1995), 'From <Bonehead> to <cLoNehEAd>: Nicknames, play and identity on Internet Relay chat', *Journal of Computer-Mediated Communication*, Vol. 1(2), http://jcmc.indiana.edu/vol1/issue2/bechar.html [accessed 28th July 2006].

Beck, U. (1992), *Risk Society: Towards a New Modernity*, Sage, London.

Becker, M.H. (1984), (ed.), *The Health Belief Model and Personal Health Behaviour*, Charles B. Slack, Thorofare, New Jersey.

Béjin, A. (1986), 'The Influence of the Sexologists and Sexual Democracy', in P. Ariès and A. Béjin (eds), *Western Sexuality: Practice and Precept in Past and Present Times*, Basil Blackwell, Oxford.

Benson, C. (1998), *Violence Against Female Prostitutes*, Department of Social Sciences, Loughborough University.

Berger, J. (1972), *Ways of Seeing*, Harmondsworth, Penguin.

Billig, M. (2001), 'Humor and Embarrassment. Limit of "nice-guy" theories of social life', *Theory, Culture and Society*, Vol. 18(5), pp. 23-43.

Bishop, R. and Robinson, L.S. (1998), *Night Market: Sexual Cultures and the Thai Economic Miracle*, Routledge, London.

Black, P. and Sharma, U. (2001), 'Men are real, women are "made up": beauty therapy and the construction of femininity', *The Sociological Review*, Vol. 49, pp. 100-116.

Blanchard, K. (1994) 'Young Johns', *Mademoiselle*, 100(5).

Bordo, S. (1993), *Unbearable Weight: Feminism, Western Culture, and the Body*, University of California Press, Berkley.

Brannon, R. and David, D. (eds), (1976), *The Forty-Nine Percent Majority*, Addison-Wesley, Reading, Mass.

Braun, V., Gavey, N. and McPhillips, K. (2003), 'The "Fair Deal"? Unpacking Accounts of Reciprocity in Heterosex', *Sexualities*, Vol. 6(2), pp. 237-61.

Brewis, J. and Linstead, S. (2000), *Sex, Work and Sex Work: Eroticizing organization*, Routledge, London.

Brewis, J. and Linstead, S. (2002), 'Managing the Sex Industry', *Culture and Organisation*, Vol. 8(4), pp. 307-26.

British Sociological Association (2005), *Equality and Ethics*, http://www.britsoc.co.uk/ [accessed 28th June 2006].

Britton, C. (1998), '"Feeling letdown": An exploration of an embodied sensation associated with breastfeeding', in S. Nettleton and J. Watson, (eds), *The Body in Everyday Life*, Routledge, London.

Brod, H. (1990), 'Pornography and the alienation of male sexuality', in J. Hearn and D. Morgan (eds), *Men, Masculinities and Social Theory*, Unwin Hyman, London.

Brown, L. (2000), *Sex Slaves: The trafficking of women in Asia*, Virago Press, London.

Bruner, J. (1987), 'Life as Narrative', *Social Research*, Vol. 54(1), pp. 11-32.

Butcher, K. (1994), 'Feminists, Prostitutes and HIV', in L. Doyal, J. Naidoo and T. Wilton, (eds), *AIDS: Setting a Feminist Agenda*, Taylor & Francis, London, pp. 151-158.

Butler, J. (1990), *Gender Trouble: Feminism and the Subversion of Identity*, Routledge, London.

Butterworth, D. (1993), 'Wanking in Cyberspace', *Trouble & Strife*, Vol. 27, Winter, pp. 33-7.

Campbell, R. (1998), 'Invisible Men: Making Visible Male Clients of Female Prostitution', in J.E. Elias, V.L. Bullough, V. Elias and G. Brewer, (eds), *Prostitution: On Whores, Hustlers, and Johns*, Prometheus Books, New York.

Chapkis, W. (1985), *Beauty Secrets*, Women's Press, London.

Chapkis, W. (1997), *Live Sex Acts: Women Performing Erotic Labour*, Cassell, London.

Chapple, A. and Ziebland, S. (2004), 'The Role of Humour for Men with Testicular Cancer', *Qualitative Health Research*, Vol. 14(8), pp. 1123-39.

Charles, N. and Kerr, M. (1986) 'Food for feminist thought', *The Sociological Review*, Vol. 34(3), pp.537-72.

Churchill, R., Allen, J., Denman, S., Willams, D., Fielding. K. and von Fragstein, M. (2000), 'Do the attitudes and beliefs of young teenagers towards general practice influence actual consultation behaviour?', *British Journal of General Practice*, Vol. 50(461), pp. 953-57.

Coffey, A., Holbrook B. and Atkinson, P. (1996), 'Qualitative Data Analysis: Technologies and Representations', *Sociological Research Online*, Vol. 1(1), http://www.socresonline.org.uk/1/1/4.html#top [accessed 28th June 2006].

Cooley, C.H. (1964) [1902], *Human Nature and the Social Order*, Charles Scribners Sons, New York.

Davies, K. (1996), 'Capturing Women's Lives: a discussion of time and methodological issues', *Women's Studies International Forum*, Vol. 19(6), pp. 579-88.

Department of Health (DoH) (2001), *The National Strategy for Sexual Health and HIV*, DoH, London.

Diamond, J. (1991), *The Rise and Fall of the Third Chimpanzee*, Radius, London.

Doherty, L., Fenton K.A., Jones, J., Paine, T.C., Higgins, S.P., Williams, D. and Palfreeman, A. (2002), 'Syphilis: old problem, new strategy', *British Medical Journal*, Vol. 325, pp. 153-56.

Douglas, M. (1966), *Purity and Danger*, Routledge, London.

Downe, P. (1999), 'Laughing When it Hurts: Humour and Violence in the Lives of Costa Rican Prostitutes', *Women's Studies International Forum*, Vol. 22, pp. 63-78.

Drake, S., Taylor, S., Brown, D. and Pillay, D. (2000), 'Improving the care of patients with genital herpes', *British Medical Journal*, Vol. 321, pp. 619-23.

Drobler, C. (1991), *Women at Work: Reader for the 1st European Prostitutes Conference*, Frankfurt, 16-18 October 1992, H.W.G., Frankfurt.

Dworkin, A. (1981), *Pornography: Men Possessing Women*, Women's Press, London.

Earle, S. and Evans, J. (2004), *Sexual Health Services in Primary Care*. Final Report presented to the Vale of Aylesbury PCT, Chiltern & South Bucks PCT, Wycombe PCT.

Ecstavasia, A. (1994), 'Fucking (with theory) for money: towards an introduction of escort prostitution', in E. Amiran and J. Unsworth (eds), *Essays in Postmodern Culture*, Oxford University Press, Oxford.

Edwards, S.S.M. (1993) 'Selling the Body, Keeping the Soul: Sexuality, Power, the Theories and Realities of Prostitution', in S. Scott and D. Morgan (eds), *Body Matters*, The Falmer Press, London.

Ehrenreich, B., Hess, E. and Jacobs G. (1986), *Remaking Love: The Feminization of Sex*, Anchor Press, New York.

Fairhurst, E. (1998), '"Growing old gracefully" as opposed to "mutton dressed as lamb": the social construction of recognising older women', in S. Nettleton and J. Watson (eds), *The Body in Everyday Life*, Routledge, London.

Faugier, J., Hayes, C. and Butterworth, C. (1992), *Drug Using Prostitutes: Their Health Care Needs and Their Clients*, University of Manchester, Manchester.

Featherstone, M. (1982), 'The Body in Consumer Culture', *Theory, Culture and Society*, Vol. 1, pp. 18-33.

Fischer, H.C. and Dubois, E.X. (1937), *Sexual Life During the World War*, Francis Aldor, London.

Flood, M. (2003), 'Lust, trust and latex: why young heterosexual men do not use condoms', *Culture, Health & Sexuality*, Vol. 5(4), pp. 353-69.

Foucault, M. (1978), *The History of Sexuality: An Introduction, Vol. 1*, Penguin, London.

Fox, N. (1999), 'Power, control and resistance in the timing of health and care', *Social Science & Medicine*, Vol. 48, pp. 1307-319.

Fox, N. and Roberts, C. (1999), 'GPs in cyberspace: the sociology of a "virtual community"', *Sociological Review*, Vol. 47, pp. 643-71.

Frank, K. (2002), *G-Strings and Sympathy: Strip Club Regulars and Male Desire*, Duke University Press, Durham.

Freund, P.E.S. and Maguire, M.B. (1999), *Health, Illness, and the Social Body: A Critical Introduction*, 3e, Prentice Hall, London.

Gagnon, J.H. and Simon, W. (1987), 'The Sexual Scripting of Oral Genital Contacts', *Archives of Sexual Behavior*, Vol. 16, pp. 1-25.

Gavey, N., McPhillips, K. and Braun, V. (1999), 'Interruptus Coitus: Heterosexuals Accounting for Intercourse', *Sexualities*, Vol. 2(1), pp. 35-68.

Gemme, R.A., Murphy, M., Bourque, M.A., Nemeh, D., and Payment, N. (1984), 'A report on prostitution in Quebec', *Working Papers on Prostitution and Pornography, Report No. 11*, Ottawa, Department of Justice.

Giddens, A. (1991), *Modernity and Self-Identity: Self and Society in the Late Modern Age*, Polity Press, Cambridge.

Giddens, A. (1992), *The Transformation of Intimacy: Sexuality, Love and Eroticism in Modern Societies*, Polity, Cambridge.

Gilfoyle, J., Wilson, J. and Brown (1992), 'Sex, Organs and Audiotape: A Discourse Analytic Approach to Talking about Heterosexual Sex and Relationships', *Feminism & Psychology*, Vol. 2(2), pp. 209-30.

Goffman, E. (1952), 'On Cooling the Mark Out: Some Aspects of Adaptation to Failure', *Psychiatry*, Vol. 15, pp. 451-63.

Goffman, E. (1959), *The Presentation of Self in Everyday* Life, Doubleday Anchor, New York.

Goffman, E. (1963), *Stigma: Notes on the Management of Spoiled Identity*, Prentice Hall, New Jersey.

Gottlieb, S. (2003) 'Oral Sex may transmit HIV', News Roundup, *British Medical Journal*, Vol. 326, p. 730.

Greer, G. (1999), *The Whole Woman*, Doubleday, London.

Grimshaw, J. (1999), 'Working out with Merleau-Ponty' in J. Arthurs and J. Grimshaw (eds), *Women's bodies: discipline and transgression*, Cassell, London.

Grosz, E. (1993), 'Bodies and knowledge: feminism and the crisis of reason', in L. Alcoff and E. Potter (eds), *Feminist Epistemologies*, Routledge, New York.

Grosz, E. (1999), 'Space, Time, and Bodies', in J. Wolmark (ed.), *Cybersexualities: A Reader on Feminist Theory, Cyborgs and Cyberspace*, Edinburgh University Press, Edinburgh.

Health Protection Agency (HPA) (2004), 'Gonorrhoea in England, Wales and Northern Ireland, Sexually Transmitted Infections Quarterly Report', *Communicable Disease Report Weekly*, Vol. 14(16), 29 April, pp. 1-6.

Henderson, T. (1999), *Disorderly Women in Eighteenth-Century London: Prostitution and Control in the Metropolis, 1730-1830*, Longman, London.

Hester, N. and Westmarland, N. (2004), *Tackling Street Prostitution: Towards a Holistic Approach*, Home Office, London.

Hewson, C., Yule, P., Laurent, D. and Vogel, C. (2003), *Internet Research Methods: a practical guide for the social and behavioural sciences*, Sage, London.

Hill Collins, P. (1990), *Black Feminist Thought: Knowledge, Consciousness and the Politics of Empowerment*, Routledge, New York.

Hine, C. and Eve, J. (1998), 'Privacy in the Marketplace', *Information Society*, Vol. 14, pp. 253-262.

Hite, S. (1988), *Women and Love: A Cultural Revolution in Progress*, Viking, London.

Hochschild, A.R. (1979), 'Emotion work, feeling rules and social structure', *American Journal of Sociology*, Vol. 85(3), pp. 551-75.

Hochschild, A.R. (1983), *The Managed Heart: The Commercialisation of Human Feelings*, University of California Press, London.

Holland, J., Ramazanoglu, C. and Scott, S. (1990), 'AIDS: From Panic Stations to Power Relations Sociological Perspectives and Problems', *Sociology*, Vol. 25(3), pp. 499-518.

Holland, J., Ramazanoglu, C., Scott, S., Sharpe, S. and Thomson, R. (1991), 'Between embarrassment and trust: Young women and the diversity of condom use', in P. Aggleton, G. Hart and P. Davies, (eds), *AIDS: Responses, interventions and care*, The Falmer Press, London.

Holland, J., Ramazanoglu, C., Sharpe, S. and Thomson, R. (1994) 'Power and Desire: The Embodiment of Female Sexuality', *Feminist Review*, 46(Spring), pp. 21-38.

Holland, J., Ramazanoglu, C., Sharpe, S. and Thomson, R. (1998), *The Male in the Head: young people, heterosexuality and power*, Tufnell Press, London.

Holzman, J. and Pine, S. (1982), 'Buying Sex: The Phenomenology of Being a John', *Deviant Behavior*, Vol. 4, pp. 89-116.

Hughes, G., Catchpole, M., Rogers, P.A., Brady, A.R., Kinghorn, G. and Thin, N. (2000), 'Comparison of risk factors for sexually transmitted infections: results from a study of attenders at three genito-urinary medicine clinics in England', *Sexually Transmitted Infections*, Vol. 76, pp. 262-67.

Humphreys, L. (1970), *Tea Room Trade: Impersonal sex in public places*, Aldine, Chicago.

Illingworth, N. (2001), 'The Internet Matters: Exploring the Use of the Internet as a Research Tool', *Sociological Research Online*, Vol. 6(2), http://www.socresonline.org.uk/6/2/illingworth.html [accessed 28th June 2006].

ITV (1998) *VICE: The Sex Trade*, November.

Jackson, M. (1984), 'Sex research and the construction of sexuality: A tool of male supremacy?', *Women's Studies International Forum*, Vol. 7(1), pp. 43-51.

Jackson, S. (1993), 'Even sociologists fall in love: An exploration in the sociology of emotions', *Sociology*, Vol. 27, pp. 201-20.

Jamieson, L. (1998), *Intimacy: Personal Relationships in Modern Societies*, Polity, Cambridge.

Jeffreys, S. (1997), *The Idea of Prostitution*, Spinifex Press, Melbourne, Australia.

Jenkins, R. (1996), *Social Identity*, Routledge, London.

Jewkes, Y. and Sharp, K. (2003), 'Crime, deviance and the disembodied self: transcending the dangers of corporeality', in Y. Jewkes, (ed.), Dot.Cons: Crime, deviance *and identity on the internet*, Willan, Devon.

Johnson, A. and Mercer, C. (2001), 'Sexual behaviour in Britain: partnerships, practices and HIV risk behaviour', *Lancet*, Vol. 358, pp. 1835-42.

Jones, R.K. (2000), 'The Unsolicited Diary as a Qualitative Research Tool for Advanced Research Capacity in the Field of Health and Illness', *Qualitative Health Research*, Vol. 10(4), pp. 555-67.

Jones, S.G. (ed.), (1999), *Doing Internet Research. Critical Issues and Methods for Examining the Net*, Sage London.

Jordan, B. (2004), *Sex, Money and Power: The Transformation of Collective Life*, Polity, Cambridge.

Jordan, T. (2001), 'Language and libertarianism: the politics of cyberculture and the culture of cyberpolitics', *The Sociological Review*, Vol. 49(1), pp. 1-17.

Kehily, M.J. (2001), 'Bodies in School: Young Men, Embodiment, and Heterosexual Masculinities', *Men and Masculinities*, Vol. 4(2), pp. 173-85.

Kehily, M.J. and Nayak, A. (1997), '"Lads and laughter": Humour and the production of sexual hierarchies', *Gender and Education*, Vol. 9(1), pp. 69-88.

Kelle, U. (1997), 'Theory Building in Qualitative Reearch and Computer Programs for the management of Textual Data', *Sociological Research Online*, Vol. 2(2) http://www.socresonline.org.uk/2/2/1.html [accessed 28th June 2006].

Kelle, U. (ed.), (1995), *Computer- Aided Qualitative Data Analysis: Theory, Methods and Practice*, Sage, London.

Keogh, M. with Harrington, J. (2003), *Survivor: Memoirs of a Prostitute*, Maverick, Co., Meath.

Kibby, M. and Costello, B. (1999), 'Displaying the Phallus: Masculinity and the Performance of Sexuality on the Internet', *Men and Masculinities*, Vol. 1(4), pp. 352-64.

Kimmel, M. (1990), 'After fifteen years: the impact of the sociology of masculinity on the masculinity of sociology', in J. Hearn and D. Morgan (eds), *Men, Masculinities and Social Theory*, Unwin Hyman, London.

Kinghorn, G. (2001), 'A sexual health & HIV strategy for England', *British Medical Journal*, Vol. 323, pp. 243-44.

Kinnell, H. (1989), *Prostitutes, their clients, and risks of female prostitutes in Birmingham, England*, Occasional Paper, Birmingham Department of Public Health.

Kinsey, A.C. (1998) [1948], *Sexual Behavior in the Human Male*, Indiana University Press, IN.

Kippax, S. and Smith, G. (2001), 'Anal Intercourse and Power in Sex Between Men', *Sexualities*, Vol. 4(4), pp. 413-34.

Kitzinger, J. (1994), 'Visible and Invisible Women in AIDS Discourses', in L. Doyal, J. Naidoo and T. Wilton, (eds), *AIDS: Setting a Feminist Agenda*, Taylor & Francis, London, pp. 95-109.

Lacey, C.J.N., Merrick, D.W., Bensley, D.C. and Fairley, I. (1997), 'Analysis of the socio-demography of gonorrhoea in Leeds, 1989-93', *British Medical Journal*, Vol. 314, pp. 1715-18.

Laurindo da Silva, L. (1999), 'Travestis and Gigolos: Male Sex Work and HIV Prevention in France', in P. Aggleton, (ed.), *Men Who Sell Sex: International perspectives on male prostitution and HIV/AIDS*, UCL Press, London, pp. 41-60.

Lee, R.M. and Fielding, N.G. (1995), '"Users" Experiences of Qualitative Data Analysis Software', in U. Kelle (ed.), *Computer-Aided Qualitative Data Analysis: Theory, Methods and Practice*, Sage, London.

Letherby, G. and Marchbank, J. (2003), 'Cyber-chattels: buying brides and babies on the Net', in Y. Jewkes (ed.), *Dot.Cons: Crime, deviance and identity on the internet*, Willan, Cullompton.

Lever, J. and Dolnick, D. (2000), 'Clients and Call Girls: Seeking Sex and Intimacy', in R. Weitzer, (ed.), *Sex for Sale: Prostitution, Pornography, and the Sex Industry*, Routledge, London.

Lever, J. and Dolnick, D. (2000), 'Clients and Call Girls: Seeking Sex and Intimacy', in R. Weitzer (ed.), *Sex for Sale: Prostitution, Pornography, and the Sex Industry*, Routledge, London.

Lopate, P. (1994), 'Portrait of my body', in L. Goldstein (ed.), *The Male Body: Features, destinies, exposures*, University of Michigan Press, Ann Arbor.

Louie, R., Crofts, N., Pyett, P. and Snow, J. (1998), *Project Client Call: Men who pay for sex in Victoria*, McFarlane Burnet Centre for Medical Research: unpublished report.

MacKinnon, C.A. (1995), 'Vindication and resistance: A response to the Carnegie Mellon study of pornography in cyberspace', *The Georgetown Law Journal*, Vol. 83(5), pp. 1959-67.

MacSween, M. (1993), *Anorexic Bodies: A feminist and sociological perspective on anorexia nervosa*, Routledge, London.

Malarek, V. (2003), *The Natashas: The New Global Sex Trade*, Viking, Ontario.

Mann, C. and Stewart, F. (2000), *Internet Communication and Qualitative Research: A Handbook for Researching Online*, Sage, London.

Månsson, S.A. (1995), 'International prostitution and traffic in persons from a Swedish perspective', in M. Klap et al. (eds), *Combating Traffic in Persons*, Utrecht: SIM Special No. 17.

Marshall, H. (1996), 'Our Bodies Ourselves: Why We Should Add Old Fashioned Empirical Phenomenology to the New Theories of the Body', *Women's Studies International Forum*, Vol. 19(3), pp. 253-265.

Martin, E. (1989), *The Woman in the Body: A Cultural Analysis of Reproduction*, Open University Press, Buckingham.

Maurer, D. (1940), *The Big Con*, Bobbs-Merrill, Indianapolis.

Mazo-Karras, R. (1989), 'The regulation of brothels in later Medieval England', *SIGNS: Journal of Women in Culture and Society*, Vol. 14(3), pp. 399-433.

McKeganey, N. (1994), 'Why do men buy sex and what are their assessments of the HIV-related risks when they do?', *AIDS Care*, Vol. 6(3), pp. 289-302.

McKeganey, N. and Barnard, M. (1996), *Sex work on the streets: Prostitutes and their clients*, Open University Press, Buckingham.

McPhillips, K., Braun, V. and Gavey, N. (2001), 'Defining (Hetero)Sex: How Imperative is the "Coital Imperative"?', *Women's Studies International Forum*, Vol. 24(2), pp. 229-40.

Mead, G.H. (1934), *Mind, Self, and Society: From the standpoint of a social behaviourist*, University of Chicago Press, London.

Mehta, M.D. and Plaza, D.E. (1997), 'Pornography in Cyberspace: An Exploration of What's in USENET', in S. Kiesler, (ed.), *Culture of the Internet*, Lawrence Erlbaum Associates, Mahwah, NJ.

Meltzer, B.N., Petras, J.W. and Reynolds, L.T. (1975), *Symbolic interactionism: Genesis, varieties and criticism*, Routledge and Kegan Paul, London.

Millstead, R. and Frith, H. (2003), 'Large-Breasted: Women Negotiating Embodiment', *Women's Studies International Forum*, Vol. 26(5), pp.455-65.

Milner, C. and Milner, R. (1972), *Black Players: The Secret World of Black Pimps*, Little Brown, Boston.

Mistress, L. (2001), 'A Faustian Bargain: Speaking out against the media', *Feminist Review*, Vol. 67, pp. 145-50.

Monto, M.A. (2000), 'Why Men Seek out Prostitutes', in R. Weitzer, (ed.), *Sex for Sale: Prostitution, Pornography, and the Sex Industry*, Routledge, London.

Monto, M.A. (2001), 'Prostitution and fellatio', *Journal of Sex Research*, Vol. 38, pp. 140-45.

Monto, M. and Hotaling, N. (2001), 'Predictors of Rape Myth Acceptance Among Male Clients of Female Street Prostitution', *Violence Against Women*, Vol. 7, pp. 275-293.

Morris, L.A. (1997), *The Male Heterosexual: Lust in His Loins, Sin in His Soul?*, Sage, London.

Nelson, J. (1985), 'Male sexuality and masculine spirituality', *Siecus Report*, Vol. 13, pp. 1-4.

Nicholson, P. (1993), 'Public Value and Private Beliefs: Why Do Women Refer Themselves for Sex Therapy?' in J.M. Ussher and C.D. Baker (eds), *Psychological Perspectives on Sexual Problems: New Directions in Theory and Practice*, Routledge, London.

Nicolson, P. and Burr, J. (2003), 'What is "normal" about women's (hetero)sexual desire and orgasm?: a report of an in-depth interview study', *Social Science & Medicine*, Vol. 57(9), pp. 1735-45.

O'Connell Davidson J. (1996), 'Prostitution and the Contours of Control', in J. Weeks and J. Holland (eds), *Sexual Cultures: Communities, Values and Intimacy*, St Martin's Press, New York.

O'Connell Davidson, J. (1995), 'The anatomy of "free choice" prostitution', *Gender, Work and Organization*, Vol. 2(1), pp. 1-10.

O'Connell Davidson, J. (1998), *Prostitution, Power and Freedom*, Polity, Oxford.

O'Neill, M. (2001), *Prostitution & Feminism: Towards a Politics of Feeling*, Polity, Oxford.

Oerton, S. and Phoenix, J. (2001), 'Sex/Bodywork: Discourses and Practices', *Sexualities*, Vol. 4(4), pp. 387–412.

Palmer, N.B. (2004), '"Let's Talk About Sex, Baby": Community-Based HIV Prevention Work and the Problem of Sex', *Archives of Sexual Behaviour*, Vol. 33(3), pp. 271-75.

Pasko, L. (2002), 'Naked Power: The Practice of Stripping as a Confidence Game', *Sexualities*, Vol. 5(1), pp. 49-66.

Patton, C. (1994), *Last Served? Gendering the HIV Pandemic*, Taylor & Francis, London.

Patton, W. and Mannison, M. (1998), 'Beyond learning to endure: Women's acknowledgement of coercive sexuality, *Women's Studies International Forum*, Vol. 21(1), pp. 31-40.

Pederson, W. and Hegna, K. (2003), 'Children and adolescents who sell sex: a community study', *Social Science & Medicine*, Vol. 56(1), pp. 135-47.

Perkins, R. (1991), *Working Girls: Prostitutes, their life and social control*, Australian Institute of Criminology, Canberra.

Perkins, R. and Bennett, G. (1985), *Being a Prostitute: Prostitute women and prostitute men*, Allen & Unwin, London.

Petchey, R., Farnsworth, W. and Heron, T. (2001), 'The maintenance of confidentiality in primary care: a survey of policies and procedures', *AIDS Care*, Vol. 13(2), pp. 251-56.

Pheterson, G. (1993), 'The whore stigma: female dishonour and male unworthiness', *Social Text*, Vol. 37, pp. 39-54.

Phoenix, J. (2000), 'Prostitute Identities: Men, Money and Violence', *British Journal of Criminology*, Vol. 40(1), pp. 37-55.

Pitts, M.K., Smith, A.M.A., Grierson, J., O'Brien, M. and Misson, S. (2004), 'Who Pays for Sex and Why? An Analysis of Social and Motivational Factors Associated With Male Clients of Sex Workers', *Archives of Sexual Behaviour*, Vol. 33(4), pp. 353-58.

Plant, S. (2000), 'On the matrix: cyberfeminist simulations', in D. Bell and B.M. Kennedy (eds), *The Cybercultures Reader*, Routledge, London.

Plummer, K. (1975), *Sexual Stigma: an interactionist account*, Routledge, London.

Plummer, K. (1983), *Documents of Life*, Allen and Unwin, London.

Plummer, K. (1996), 'Intimate Citizenship and the Culture of Sexual Storytelling', in J. Weeks and J. Holland (eds), *Sexual Cultures: Communities, Values and Intimacy*, Macmillan, London.

Plumridge, E. (2001), 'Rhetoric, reality and risk outcomes in sex work', *Health, Risk & Society*, Vol. 3(2), pp. 199-215.

Plumridge, E. and Chetwynd, S.J. (1996), 'Patrons of the Sex Industry: Perceptions of Risk', *AIDS Care*, Vol. 8(4), pp. 405-417.

Plumridge, E., Chetwynd, J., Reed, A. and Gifford, S. (1997), 'Discourses of emotionality in commercial sex: the missing client voice', *Feminism & Psychology*, Vol. 7, pp. 228-43.

Poster, M. (1995), 'Postmodern Virtualities', in M. Featherstone and R. Burrows (eds), *Cyberspace/Cyberbodies/Cyberpunk: Cultures of Technological Embodiment*, Sage, London.

Potts, A. (2000), 'Coming, Coming, Gone: A Feminist Deconstruction of Heterosexual Orgasm', *Sexualities*, Vol. 3(1), pp. 55-76.

Potts, A. (2001), 'The Man with Two Brains: hegemonic masculine subjectivity and the discursive construction of the unreasonable penis-self', *Journal of Gender Studies*, Vol. 10(2), pp. 145-56.

Price, J. (1988) *Motherhood: What it does to your mind*, Pandora, London.

Pyett, P. and Warr, D. (1997), 'Vulnerability on the streets: female sex workers and HIV risk', *AIDS Care*, Vol. 9(5), pp. 539-547.

Pyle, J.L. (2001), 'Sex, Maids, and Export Processing: Risks and Reasons for Gendered Global Production Networks', *International Journal of Politics, Culture and Society*, Vol. 15(1), pp. 55-76.

Quaife, G.R. (1979), *Wanton Wenches and Wayward Wives: Peasants and Illicit Sex in Early Seventeenth Century England*, Croom Helm, London.

Queen, C. (2000), 'Towards a Taxonomy of Tricks: A Whore Considers the Age-Old Question, "What Do Client's Want?"', in M.B. Sycamore (ed.), *Tricks and Treats: Sex Workers Write About their Clients*, Hawthorn Press, London.

Raymond, J.G. (1998), 'Prostitution as violence against women: NGO stonewalling in Beijing and elsewhere', *Women's Studies International Forum*, Vol. 21(1), pp. 1-9.

Redman, P. (2001), 'The Discipline of Love: Negotiation and Regulation in Boys' Performance of a Romance-Based Heterosexual Masculinity', *Men and Masculinities*, Vol. 4(2), pp. 186-200.

Rhodes, T. (1996), 'Culture, drugs and unsafe sex: Confusion about causation', *Addiction*, Vol. 91, pp. 753-58.

Rhodes, T. and Cusick, L. (2002), 'Accounting for unprotected sex: stories of agency and acceptability', *Social Science & Medicine*, Vol. 55, pp. 211-26.

Roberts, C., Kippax, S., Waldby, C. and Crawford, J. (1995), 'Faking It. The Story of "Ohhh!"', *Women's Studies International Forum*, Vol. 18(5/6), pp. 523-32.

Robins, K. (1995), 'Cyberspace and the World We Live In', in M. Featherstone and R. Burrows, (eds), *Cyberspace/Cyberbodies/Cyberpunk: Cultures of Technological Embodiment*, Sage, London.

Ryan, J. (1994), 'Women, modernity and the city', *Theory, Culture and Society*, Vol. 11(4), pp. 35-64.

Salvadori, H. (1997), 'UK report: my life in a London brothel', *Marie Claire*, October, pp. 116-22.

Sanders, T. (2004a), 'A continuum of risk? The management of health, physical and emotional risks by female sex workers', *Sociology of Health & Illness*, Vol. 26(5), pp. 557-74.

Sanders, T. (2004b), 'Controllable Laughter: Managing Sex Work Through Humour', *Sociology*, Vol. 33(2), pp. 273-291.

Sanders, T. (2005), *Sex Work: A Risky Business*, Willan, Cullompton.

Sassatelli, R. (2003), 'Beyond Health and Beauty: A Critical perspective on Fitness Culture' in G. Boswell and F. Poland (eds), *Women's Minds, Women's Bodies: An Interdisciplinary Approach to Women's Health*, Palgrave, Basingstoke.

Scambler, G. (1997), 'Conspicuous and inconspicuous sex work: The neglect of the ordinary and mundane', in G. Scambler and A. Scambler, (eds), *Rethinking Prostitution: Purchasing Sex in the 1990s*, Routledge, London.

Scambler, G. and Scambler, A. (1997), (eds), *Rethinking Prostitution: Purchasing Sex in the 1990s*, Routledge, London.

Scott, J. (2003), 'Prostitution and public health in New South Wales', *Culture, Health & Sexuality*, Vol. 5(3), pp. 277-93.

Segal, L. (1997), *Slow Motion*, Virago Press, London.

Seidler, V.J. (1989), *Rediscovering Masculinity: Reason, Language and Sexuality*, Routledge, London.

Sharp, K. and Earle, S. (2003), 'Cyberpunters and cyberwhores', in Y. Jewkes (ed.), *Dot. Cons: Crime, deviance and identity on the internet*, Willan, Cullompton.

Sijuwade, P.O. (1995), 'Counterfeit intimacy: A dramaturgical analysis of an erotic performance', *Social Behaviour and Personality*, Vol. 23(4), pp. 369-76.

Simmons, M. (1998), 'Theorizing Prostitution: The Question of Agency', in B.M. Dank and R. Refinetti (eds), *Sex Work & Sex Workers, Sexuality & Culture, Vol. 2*, Transaction Publishers, London.

Skidmore, D. and Hayter, E. (2000), 'Risk and sex: ego-centricity and sexual behaviour in young adults', *Health, Risk & Society*, Vol. 2(1), pp. 23-32.

Smith, C. (1999), 'Talking Dirty in "For Women" Magazine', J. Arthurs and J. Grimshaw (eds), *Women's bodies: discipline and transgression*, Cassell, London.

Soothill, K. and Sanders, T. (2005), 'The Geographical Mobility, Preferences and Pleasures of Prolific Punters: A Demonstration Study of the Activities of Prostitutes', *Sociological Research Online*, Vol. 10(1), http://www.socresonline. org.uk/10/1/soothill.html [accessed 28th June 2006].

Spence, D. (1982), *Narrative Truth and Historical Truth*, Norton, New York.

Spencer, L., Faulkner, A. and Keegan, J. (1988), *Talking about Sex: Asking the Public about Sexual Behaviour and Attitudes*, Social and Community Planning Research, London.

Sproull, L. and Faraj, S. (1997), 'Atheism, Sex and Databases: The Net as a Social Technology', in S. Kiesler (ed.), *Culture of the Internet*, Lawrence Erlbaum Associates, Mahwah, NJ.

Stone, A.R. (1991), 'Will the Real Body Please Stand Up: Boundary Stories About Virtual Cultures', in M. Benedikt (ed.), *Cyberspace: First Steps*, MIT Press, London.

Strasser, S. (2003), 'Introduction', in S. Strasser (ed.), *Commodifying Everything: Relationships of the Markets*, Routledge, London.

Sullivan, E. and Simon, W. (1998), 'The Client: A Social, Psychological, and Behavioural Look at the Unseen Patron of Prostitution', J.E. Elias, V.L. Bullough, V. Elias and G. Brewer, (eds), *Prostitution: On Whores, Hustlers, and Johns*, Prometheus Books, New York.

Sullivan, L.J. (1997), 'Cyberbabes: (Self-) Representation of Women and the Virtual Male Gaze', *Computers and Composition*, Vol. 14, pp. 189-204.

Taormino, T. (1998), *The Ultimate Guide to Anal Sex for Women*, Cleis Press, San Francisco, CA.

Tavella, P. (1992), 'Long Climb to the Peak', *Connexions*, Vol. 38, pp. 2-3.

Taylor, D. (2006), 'Sex workers are a soft target in the asylum figures battle', *The Guardian*, Thursday June 22 http://www.guardian.co.uk/commentisfree/story/0,,1802914,00.html [accessed 28th June 2006].

The UK Collaborative Group for HIV and STI Surveillance (2004), *Focus on Prevention. HIV and other Sexually Transmitted Infections in the United Kingdom in 2003*, Health Protection Agency Centre for Infections: London.

Thorogood, N. (2000), 'Mouthrules and the Construction of Sexual Identities', *Sexualities*, Vol. 3(2), pp. 165-82.

Tiefer, L. (1995), *Sex Is Not A Natural Act & Other Essays*, Westview Press, Oxford.

Tomlinson, J. (1998), 'ABC of Sexual Health: Taking a sexual history', *British Medical Journal*, Vol. 317, pp. 1573-6.

Turkle, S. (1995), *Life on the Screen*, Simon and Schuster, New York.

Turkle, S. (1997), 'Constructions and Reconstructions of Self in Virtual Reality: Playing in the MUDS', in S. Kiesler (ed.), *Culture of the Internet*, Lawrence Erlbaum Associates, Mahwah, NJ.

Urla, J. and Swedlund, A.C. (1998), 'The Anthropometry of Barbie: Unsettling Ideals of the Feminine Body in Popular Culture', in J. Terry and J. Urla (eds), *Deviant Bodies: Critical Perspectives in Science and Popular Culture*.

van Zoonen, L. (2002), 'Gendering the Internet: claims, controversies and cultures', *European Journal of Communication*, Vol. 17(1), pp. 5-23.

Vance, C.S. (1984), 'Pleasure and Danger: Towards a Politics of Sexuality', in C.S. Vance (ed.), *Pleasure and Danger: Exploring Female Sexuality*, Routledge, London.

Vannini, P. and McCright, A.M. (2004), 'To Die For: The Semiotic Seductive Power of the Tanned Body', *Symbolic Interaction*, Vol. 27(3), pp. 309-32.

Vanwesenbeeck, I., de Graff, R., Van Zessen, G. and Straver, C. and Visser, J. H. (1993), 'Protection Styles of Prostitutes Clients: Intentions, behaviour and considerations in relation to AIDS', *Journal of Sex Education and Therapy*, Vol. 19(2), pp. 79-92.

Vitellone, N. (2000), 'Condoms and the Making of "Testosterone Man"', *Men and Masculinities*, Vol. 3(2), pp. 152-67.

Walker, A. (1981), *You Can't Keep a Good Woman Down*, Harcourt Brace Jorvanovich, New York.

Walkowitz, J. (1980), *Prostitution and Victorian Society*, Cambridge University Press, Cambridge.

Warr, D.J. (2001), 'The importance of love and understanding: Speculation on romance in safe sex', *Women's Studies International Forum*, Vol. 24(2), pp. 241-52.

Warr, D.J. and Pyett, P.M. (1999), 'Difficult relations: sex work, love and intimacy', *Sociology of Health & Illness*, Vol. 21(3), pp. 290-309.

Weatherall, A. and Priestley, A. (2001), 'A Feminist Discourse Analysis of Sex "Work"', *Feminism & Psychology*, Vol. 11(3), pp. 323-40.

Weitzer, R. (2000), *Sex for Sale*, Routledge, London.

Wellings, K., Field, J., Johnson, A.M., Wadsworth, J. and Bradshaw, S. (1994), *Sexual Behaviour in Britain: the National Survey of Sexual Attitudes and Lifestyles*, Penguin, London.

Whitehead, S.M. (2002), *Men and Masculinities: Key Themes and New Directions*, Polity, Oxford.

Whittaker, D. and Hart, G. (1996), 'Research note: managing risks: the social organisation of indoor sex work', *Sociology of Health & Illness*, Vol. 18(3), pp. 399-414.

Wilton, T. (1994), 'Feminism and the Erotics of Health Promotion', in L. Doyal, J. Naidoo and T. Wilton (eds), *AIDS: Setting a Feminist Agenda*, Taylor & Francis, London.

Wilton, T. (1999), 'Selling Sex, Giving Care: The Construction of AIDS as a Workplace Hazard', in N. Daykin and L. Doyal, (eds), *Health and Work: Critical Perspectives*, Macmillan, London.

Wojcicki, J.M. and Malala, J. (2001), 'Condom use, power and HIV/AIDS risk: sex-workers bargain for survival in Hillbrow/Joubert Park/Berea, Johannesburg', *Social Science & Medicine*, Vol. 53(1), pp. 99-121.

Wood, E.A. (2000), 'Working in the Fantasy Factory: The Attention Hypothesis and the Enacting of Masculine Power in Strip Clubs, *Journal of Contemporary Ethnography*, Vol. 29(1), pp. 5-31.

Woodward, K. (2003), 'Representations of Motherhood', in S. Earle and G. Letherby (eds), *Gender, Identity and Reproduction: social perspectives*, Palgrave, London.

Worsnop, J. (1990), 'A re-evaluation of "the problem of surplus women" in 19th century England, the case of the 1851 Census', *Women's Studies International Forum*, Vol. 13(1/2), pp. 21-31.

Wyatt Seal, D. and Ehrhardt, A.A. (2003), 'Masculinity and urban men: perceived scripts for courtship, romantic, and sexual interactions with women', *Culture, Health & Sexuality*, Vol. 5(4), pp. 295-319.

Index